GOD AND HISTORY
IN THE OLD TESTAMENT

RELEASE

BY HARVEY H. GUTHRIE, JR.

God and History
in the Old Testament

ST. JOSEPH'S UNIVERSITY   STX
BS1171.G98
God and history in the Old Testament.

3 9353 00005 4609

80272

BS1171
.G98

GREENWICH · CONNECTICUT
1960

© 1960 by THE SEABURY PRESS, INCORPORATED
Library of Congress Catalog Card Number: 60-5886
Design by NANCY H. DALE
Printed in the UNITED STATES OF AMERICA
330-860-C-3.5

TO DORIS AND
TO LARRY, LYNN,
STEPHEN, AND ANDREW

Preface

This book represents an attempt to assess what the Old Testament is about. It is my conviction that such an attempt must involve more than the mere recital of the contents of the Old Testament or an introduction to Hebrew language and thought. Such an attempt must involve the translation of the content and thought of the Old Testament into contemporary categories capable of catching something of the total import of the biblical point of view. It is for this reason that I have stressed that the Old Testament is concerned more with what would today be called a philosophy of history than with religion as currently understood in many quarters.

In successive chapters I have sought to show how all the various types of Old Testament literature, if not equally creative of such a point of view, find their meaning in terms of it. Since the chief character in the Old Testament is the living God, the discussion of the literature and the history behind it is preceded by an introduction on the biblical conception of God and on the ways in which he makes himself known. And, since the Old Testament has to do with the divine purpose undergirding a yet unfinished history, a final chapter seeks to relate the Old Testament to the New and to the present.

It is only fair to warn the reader that, while I am deeply indebted to many scholars, both the over-all point of view of this book and the reconstructions of Old Testament history it offers represent only one man's opinion. This should be emphasized particularly with regard to the historical reconstructions lest the impression be given that the solutions suggested here are the only answers to the problems. Readers familiar with Old Testament studies will recognize my dependence upon certain scholars. They will also recognize that I have struck out on my own at some points. This book makes no claim to finality. The justification for any vagaries of historical reconstruction is to be found in the demand of the Old Testament itself that the history to which it appeals be taken seriously. To seek to deal with that history is not only to attempt to satisfy contemporary canons of credibility. It is to confess loyalty to the Old Testament point of view. The notes to the various chapters, in which reference is made chiefly to widely accessible and nontechnical works, provide suggestions for checking what is said here with what others have said.

For nurture of the interest that has led to this book I am indebted to Dr. C. A. Simpson, Dean of Christ Church, Oxford. I am also indebted, in more ways than I can recount, to Professor Robert C. Dentan of the General Theological Seminary. For the final product, however, neither of them is to be blamed!

Except for one or two places where I have used my own translation, the biblical quotations are from the Revised Standard Version. For permission to use the RSV and for permission to change its text by using "Yahweh" where the Hebrew original uses the divine name I am indebted to The Standard Bible Committee of the Division of Christian Education of the National Council of the Churches of Christ. The quotation from William Temple's *Nature, Man and God* in the introduction is used by kind permission of Macmillan and Company, Ltd., and St. Martin's Press.

HARVEY H. GUTHRIE, JR.

Contents

GOD AND HISTORY
IN THE OLD TESTAMENT

Introduction

How is God found? This is the question with which, it would seem, man should begin his search for the meaning of life. As a significant answer to this question, the Bible—particularly, the Old Testament—commands attention. There are many ways in which one can approach the Old Testament. Much of it is great literature. It is also the principal source for reconstructing the history of one of the minor powers of the ancient Near East. Moreover, it is a book which must be taken into account in any attempt to deal with the history of man's religions. But the claim the Old Testament makes for itself, implicitly as well as explicitly, is that it is the witness, in literary form, of a people who knew the one true God. It is with that Old Testament claim that we shall be concerned, and it is in terms of the crucial question, How is God found? that this examination of the Old Testament is undertaken.

To find an adequate answer to any question it is necessary first to ask the proper question. In the case of the Old Testament, if we are to allow it to give its own answer, we should perhaps rephrase our question, for Israel did not so much ask, "How is God found?" as "*How* and *where* and *as whom* has God made himself known?" Israel never conceived of God as a fact, a law, a force—as something to be discovered. For Israel God was someone, and finding him depended upon his willingness to reveal himself, to make himself known. From the Old Testament point of view God cannot be found unless he is willing to make himself known, unless he chooses to take the initiative in revealing himself.

To state the matter thus, however, is to be abstract in a way the Bible is never abstract. It would be better to say that the Bible simply takes it for granted that the God who really is God has chosen to reveal himself. Taking that for granted, the Bible goes on from there. We know that knowing God involves the kind of search and the kind of discovery appropriate to knowing some *one* rather than to knowing objects or laws, precisely because God has made himself known as some *one*. In order to hear what the Bible is saying, we must have that firmly in mind.

The importance of this point lies in its implications for the way in which we approach the Bible, particularly the Old Testament. The Old Testament contains a wide variety of literature: stories, poetry, prophetic pronouncements, dramatic dialogues. Beneath them all, however, whatever be their form or specific content, this primary assumption is made: that God has reached out to make himself known and therefore our "discovery" of him is possible only because he has done that. We are not, therefore, reading the Old Testament on its own terms if we read it to discover a "truth," to search in it for right ideas or absolute laws of some kind. We miss the point if we approach the Old Testament in the way in which we would set out on a search for a lost object, an adequate theory, or a right system of doctrine. We do know something of what God is like, but we know it because he has made himself known. We may formulate some theories *about* him, but we are able to do so only because what he has done has led us to some knowledge *of* him.

This was well stated by William Temple:

. . . there is no such thing as revealed truth. There are truths of revelation, that is to say, propositions which express the results of correct thinking concerning revelation; but they are not themselves directly revealed. (*Nature, Man and God, p. 317*)

The Bible, the Old Testament, is a witness to the revelation. We must read it as such if we are truly to understand it, to hear its witness. That is why the proper questions are "*How* and *where* and *as whom* has God made himself known?" Some preliminary observations on these three questions are in order before we turn to our examination of the Old Testament itself.

THE "HOW" OF REVELATION

Living beings can never be known by means of abstract formulas or definitions, but only in concrete terms—by their words and actions, by the events in which they participate. It is one thing to describe the chemical composition or the psychological make-up of someone, but to convey a real sense of the living person, his story must be told. Generalities or abstractions will not do. So it is, from the point of view of the Old Testament, with the living God. The Old Testament does not give philosophical formulas telling us *what* God is. If we open it looking for that, we shall never hear what it is really saying. In Old Testament thinking, God is some *one,* and his story must be told if he is to be known.

For this reason a great part of the Old Testament—over half of it—is narrative. In the order in which the books appear in the English Bible, the story begins with the creation of the world, continues with a sketch of the origins of the races and nations that inhabit the world (all, of course, as the writers knew them), then proceeds to tell the story of Israel from its beginnings to its situation in the latter years of the Persian Empire. The person who turns to the Old Testament for some kind of systematic exposition of the nature of God will, inevitably, be disappointed. No such exposition is given. Rather, a story is told, the story of a particular people. And, there is no escaping it, the prejudices and limited point of view of that people are evident in many places.

The reason, however, for telling the story of this particular people is that those who tell it are convinced that in this story the *one* who is God has involved himself. It is quite clear that the story is being told as more than the reminiscences of one, little human family. In this story, Israel is convinced, God has acted, God who is some *one,* and the story has to be told if he is to be known. Those responsible for giving us the Old Testament are convinced that God, the God who really is God, has revealed himself to men. They are convinced that he has revealed himself to be some *one,* and no abstract formula can capture the uniqueness and reality of who he is. His story has to be told. And, like the stories of all persons, it is a specific story or narrative.

Furthermore, even in those places where the Old Testament does give a concise statement of its faith about God, it does not use abstract formulas. An example of such a statement is contained in the ancient *credo* now found in Deuteronomy:

> A wandering Aramean was my father; and he went down in to Egypt and sojourned there, few in number; and there he became a nation, great, mighty, and populous. And the Egyptians treated us harshly, and afflicted us, and laid upon us hard bondage. Then we cried to Yahweh the God of our fathers, and Yahweh heard our voice, and saw our affliction, our toil, and our oppression; and Yahweh brought us out of Egypt with a mighty hand and an outstretched arm, with great terror, with signs and wonders; and he brought us into this place and gave us this land, a land flowing with milk and honey. (Deuteronomy 26:5-9)

This passage makes clear certain Israelite convictions about God: God was compassionate; God was righteous; God was powerful; God was loving; God was sovereign in human history. Yet the Israelite did not know these things as abstract facts. He knew them as we know things about living beings.

He knew them in terms of what God, as the Israelite saw it, had done. The Israelite was sure that God was compassionate because of the pity with which he had regarded the plight of Israel in Egypt. The Israelite was sure that God was righteous because of the indignation with which he had regarded the maltreatment of a weaker people by a dominant power. He knew that God was powerful because of the way in which he had brought Israel out of bondage in the face of the forces of Pharaoh. He knew that God was loving because of the care he had taken to give his people a land in which to live. He knew that God was sovereign in history because, were he not, the wonderful things which the Israelite confessed could not have taken place.

Thus, the nature of the God who is God dictated the form that the witness to him had to take. For the Israelite he was some *one,* and no abstract definition of his nature could do him justice. Only the story, *his* story, could bear some kind of witness to the concrete, living *one* whose actions had been such that he must be God. It was not that the idea "God" was discovered at the end of a philosophical search. It was that some *one,* Yahweh (that is the most plausible reconstruction of the actual name), had acted in such a way that he must be God.

A great deal of the Old Testament is, therefore, narrative. It is narrative in the best sense of the word, which does not merely recount "bare events," but captures, as great narrative must, the "feel" of the events, the reality of the one who was acting in them, the response elicited by them in those who were involved in them.

Those books of the Old Testament which are not narrative —the Psalter, large sections of the prophetic books, Job, and Proverbs—are, for the most part, poetry. This is so because in these pages the writers are bearing witness to the *one* who, they are convinced, has been at work in the life that is theirs in memory and experience. This poetry is the response inspired by the *one* men found present and active in concrete, particular events of history, and its form as poetry is dictated by that to which (or to whom) it is bearing witness. For poetry does justice to living beings and living relationships in a way that bare abstract definition cannot. Accordingly, certain responses can be adequately described only in poetic forms.

How, then, does God make himself known? He makes himself known in specific acts, in particular events, in concrete things that he has done. He makes himself known in the concreteness of history, and he cannot be described in abstractions. His presence, his character, his unique reality can only be captured in the telling of a story or in the terms of poetic imagination. If we take the Old Testament seriously, he can only be found when we accept that, when we look for him in *his* story.

THE "WHERE" OF REVELATION

The Old Testament answer to our second question, "Where has God made himself known?", is also conditioned by the faith that God is some *one*. God makes himself known in the concreteness and particularity of history: that was the answer to the "How?" God makes himself known in *the* history of Israel: that is the answer to the "Where?" If we modern men, with our habit of thinking conceptually, have difficulty in accepting the Old Testament conviction that God is a specific some *one*, we have even more difficulty with the Old Testament conviction that this specific someone chose Israel.

We cannot, however, understand the Old Testament until we understand that this conviction is not only implicit on its every page, but an integral part of the view of God taken by the Old Testament. There is no question but that the Old Testament is talking about the God who is God of the whole earth. There is no question but that the God whom Israel saw present in her history is the sovereign Judge and Ruler of all history. Nevertheless, the Old Testament maintains, God has revealed that he is God by choosing a particular people and by making himself known in the events that make up their history. Why should this be so? How could God, if he is the one true God, be so exclusive?

The key to the Old Testament's conviction of God's choice of Israel is to be found in the more basic conviction that God is some *one*. And the clue to our difficulties with the biblical conviction of God's choice of Israel is to be found in our inability to accept all the implications of the faith that God is some *one*. It is hard for us to accept the view that God is not some *thing* that we, in our wisdom and sincerity and goodness, can find at the end of *our* successful search. It is hard for us to accept the fact that God is some *one* upon whom we not only depend for our very existence, but who must choose to reveal himself to us if we are to know him at all.

But if the God who really is God is some *one,* not an idea or a concept or an impersonal force, then knowing him is going to involve the same elements involved in knowing persons. It is going to involve the particularity always involved in personal relationship. And if God, as the Old Testament witnesses, has chosen to make himself known to men, then he is going to have to choose some particular place, some particular relationship, in which he may make himself known as some *one*. Had he not made such a choice, no one could know him as some *one*.

Something like that lies behind the designation of Israel as "the chosen people." We do not give the Old Testament, the book in which Israel's story is told, the place of honor that we do because of Israel's superior gifts or wisdom or virtue. We give it a place of honor because Israel was the community to which God chose to make himself known. When we would find out about the God who is some *one,* we must depend upon the testimony of those who have known him in the particularity of a relationship in history.

Why God chose Israel rather than some other people is a question only God can answer. Being a human community, Israel sometimes gave human, self-satisfied answers. More often, Israel was humbled by the mysterious, wonderful knowledge that he had chosen her. The writers of Deuteronomy, for example, saw the choice of Israel as nothing warranting self-centered pride:

> It was not because you were more in number than any other people that Yahweh set his love upon you and chose you, for you were the fewest of all peoples. (Deuteronomy 7:7)

And, rather than being egotistical about it, Amos saw God's choice of Israel as the source of a terrible, inescapable responsibility:

> You only have I known
> of all the families of the earth;
> therefore will I punish you
> for all your iniquities. (Amos 3:2)

Why God chose Israel may be an interesting question for speculation, as may be the question of whether or not he tried to make himself known in the same way elsewhere. That he chose Israel to be the community in which, through the closeness and particularity of a relationship, he would make himself known to the whole world is something so basic to the Old Testament point of view that the Old Testament cannot be understood if it be left out of the picture. Indeed, we have missed a basic part of the biblical view of the nature of God if we reject the conviction of Israel that God had chosen her. And, if Israel's faith be right, we have, by being mistaken about his nature, made a mistake that will have fundamental consequences for the success of our search for God.

God is the God of the whole world. The Old Testament is sure of that. God's purpose is a universal purpose. The Old Testament is sure of that, too. But the Old Testament is also sure that God's reign is the reign of some *one,* and that the some *one* who does reign can only be known in the particularity of the history of the community in which he has made himself known. It is, therefore, more than national pride that prompts the prophecy of Zechariah:

> In those days ten men from the nations of every tongue shall take hold of the robe of a Jew, saying, "Let us go with you, for we have heard that God is with you." (Zechariah 8:23)

The basis of that prophecy is found in the distinctive conviction of the Old Testament that God is some *one*. That that conviction is not negated but fulfilled in the New Testament is clear, for whoever knows God through Jesus Christ has, in more than a figurative sense, caught hold of the robe of a Jew.

THE "AS WHOM" OF REVELATION

The key to an answer to our third question is also found in the basic assumption of the Old Testament that God is some *one*. For the Old Testament there is no divine reality of some kind that corresponds to what *our* image of God may be. There is some *one,* given and particular and unique, who is God. Our finding God depends upon our accepting that one *as he has made himself known.*

As whom has God made himself known? The answer of the Old Testament is: As the living Lord of history and of the world in which history takes place. For Israel it was not just that some one had made himself known in her life and history. Israel maintained that the one who had made himself known to her was such that he must be the Lord of all life and history. That is the fundamental reason for Israel's telling of her story. That is what the Old Testament is all about.

So it is that the Old Testament, in a very real sense, is not a religious book at all. It may come as a shock to us who are accustomed to think of the Old Testament as the larger part of a book bound in pious black leather that the word "religion" does not occur in the Old Testament. The way in which the Old Testament answers the question, "As whom has God made himself known?", makes it more than a religious book in the narrow sense of the word "religious." The Old Testament is not an answer to some specifically religious question, but to the question of the real meaning of history. The some *one,* Yahweh who is God, is not, for ancient Israel, a "religious" figure. He is the Lord of history, the sovereign creator of all things. He is the one whose purpose is being brought to inevitable accomplishment not only in acts of piety and worship, but in the rise and fall of empires, in the inexorable onward movement of events. All of history is his story.

Thus, the faith of Israel is something other than a "religion" that offers an avenue of escape from the ambiguities of life in this world. That faith rests upon history, upon remembered events, in which it has seen some *one* revealing himself as the Lord of history. That faith holds that human history is itself, for man, the significant thing. It is in history that man lives, at every moment, under the one who, in Israel's history, has revealed himself to be God. Man's salvation is never conceived as individual disentanglement from the matrix of history. Man's salvation is involved in the arrival of history at that place to which it is the purpose of God to bring it. Israel's faith claims to provide a clue to what that purpose is—and to *whose* purpose it is.

It is for this reason that the Old Testament does not discuss religion in the usual sense of the word, but recounts the story of a people. The Old Testament bears witness to a series of remembered events in which, it is confident, the one who is Lord of history has made himself known and has been working to bring his purpose to accomplishment. It is because he has done so that those particular events are recounted. This is what is meant by the assertion that the religion of the Old Testament is not just religion, but *historical* religion. It harks back to certain events in which, it affirms, God was at work.

And the religion of the Old Testament is historical in another sense. It is not merely that ancient events were remembered and recounted because of Israel's belief that the one who is God had been at work in them. The meaning of the events of any given present was, for Israel, found in the faith that God was reigning in those events as well as in the events of the past. It is to this that the prophets most obviously bear witness. But the narratives in which the ancient events are recounted bear witness to it, too. For it was at particular times in Israel's history that the ancient traditions were written down. They came to be written because the writers were sure that the one who had revealed himself as God in the events of older times was also reigning in their own times. "We know," they were saying, "who it is who is sovereign in what is transpiring in the present because he revealed himself as sovereign in the time of our fathers." So an historical present drove them to recall the historical past in order to assert their faith that all history finds its meaning in the *one* who is Lord of history and in his purpose.

It is with this double sense of the meaning of "historical," found in the various parts of the Old Testament bearing witness to the one who is Lord of history, that we shall be concerned in the pages that follow. We shall, in terms of the insights provided by modern biblical scholarship, try to see how the Old Testament witnesses to the sovereignty of God both in terms of the ancient traditions of Israel, and in terms of the recording and application of those traditions in later ages. Having looked at various types of Old Testament literature in this way, we shall then look at the main line of Old Testament thought, attempting to relate it to its culmination in the life and thought of Jesus and the rise of the Christian Church.

CHAPTER ONE

The Witness of the Narrative

The Old Testament narrative did not originate as a series of stories told around the campfires of a primitive half-savage people. The world in which the earliest parts of the Old Testament were written was an extremely civilized and cultured world, a world with thousands of years of history behind it. It is true that the ultimate origins of Israel are to be found in the Arabian Desert. It is also true that the original home of Yahweh, the God of Israel, was somewhere in that desert and that his presence was believed to be manifest in the dread and powerful phenomena of storm and volcanic activity. Nevertheless, we misunderstand the narrative of the Old Testament and underestimate those who were responsible in the first place for that narrative, if we condescendingly view it as a collection of fanciful tales from a primitive people whose religion was chiefly characterized by naïveté.[1]

The world in which Israel emerged as a fairly important small empire, about 1000 B.C., was a world in which human civilization had existed for millennia. To the east of Palestine, northward around the edge of the Arabian Desert, lay Mesopotamia. There, in the large valley formed by the Tigris and Euphrates Rivers, the cradle of human civilization is undoubtedly to be found. To the south, down along the coast of the Mediterranean, lay Egypt, stretched threadlike along the narrow oasis formed by the Nile. Twenty dynasties of pharaohs had come to power and fallen there by the time of Saul and David, and the great pyramids and the Sphinx at Gizeh had already been standing for nearly two thousand years. To the north of Palestine, in the mountains of present-day Turkey, was the center of the Hittite empire, the richness of whose culture has been uncovered only in our own day.

Furthermore, Palestine itself had had a long history. Recent excavations at ancient Jericho have demonstrated that the site of that city was occupied by man as early as 7000 B.C., and excavations at ancient Ugarit, on the coast north of Palestine and almost directly opposite Cyprus, have shown that the culture and the religion of the Canaanites, Israel's predecessors, rivaled those of Babylonia and Egypt.[2] Even though it was a prephilosophical and prescientific world into which Israel emerged as a kingdom under Saul and David, it was not a primitive world. It was more like the world of Homer than the world of the Hottentots. Though its roots go back to desert days, the narrative of the Old Testament in its written form originated as the epic of an empire that stretched from the Mediterranean far out beyond the Jordan into the desert and from the borders of Egypt nearly up to Turkey, including modern Israel, Transjordan, and Syria. It is when we see this narrative against its historical background as such an epic and cease to think of it as a "religious" document in the modern sense of the word, that we begin to appreciate it for what it really is. It is when we compare it with the epic literature of other ancient Near Eastern kingdoms that we begin to discern the uniqueness of the Hebraic point of view.[3]

BEHIND THE NARRATIVE: PREMONARCHICAL ISRAEL

The course of events that led to the establishment of the Hebrew monarchy under Saul and David was, as history always is, complex and many-sided. Indeed, in spite of the over-simplified and foreshortened story which the Bible in its present form tells, the nature and experience of Israel before the time of Saul and David are very difficult to recover. It is clear that the later Israel was made up of different clans and tribes that had entered Palestine at varying times, each with a background of its own. It is also clear that the unity that made it possible to speak of "Israel" was something that had been achieved, for the most part, after the settlement of the land by these various tribes and clans. Furthermore, the stories of early Israel as we have them in the Old Testament were handed down to us by those who saw the early age in the light of the later unity.

A number of things, however, may be discerned as characteristic of premonarchical Israel. First of all, there were two centers around which the various clans and tribes grouped themselves. One center was in the northern part of Palestine, where apparently, first at Shechem and later at Shiloh, the tribes who traced their ancestry to Rachel and her handmaiden in the traditional genealogies had organized themselves into a tribal confederation.[4] Membership in this confederation involved loyalty to the God Yahweh and certain obligations to fight common enemies and to punish offenses on the part of other members. Indeed, the concepts of the "holy war" and of the "ban" which were invoked against certain peoples and cities undoubtedly go back to the religious obligations incumbent upon the members of this confederation. In them is expressed the conviction that those who had been called together by the God Yahweh were caught up into a purpose that moved along through the events of history, a purpose which could not be withstood by human opposition and which involved the secure establishment of Israel in her land.[5]

The members of this northern confederation bore the name "sons of Israel," or simply "Israel." The mutual bond of obligation to one another among the tribes and of absolute obligation to Yahweh was expressed in terms of *convenant,* which will be discussed in the next chapter. This premonarchical organization in north central Palestine was characterized by a vigorous, fierce, independent spirit. It was conscious of the uncompromising loyalty owed to Yahweh by his people. It was proudly aware of the favor which Yahweh had shown toward his people, and was jealous lest that awareness be lost through dilution in the culture of Canaan. The obligation owed Yahweh under the covenant was expressed in terms of the regulations given by God at a holy mountain in the desert. The power of Yahweh to protect his people was celebrated in the stories of his defeat of Israel's enemies through chosen leaders upon whom he had bestowed his spirit.[6]

The other center around which grouped the various tribes and clans that were to make up the kingdom of Saul and David appears to have been Hebron, in the extreme south of Palestine. These were, chiefly, the tribes and clans which traced their ancestry to Leah and her handmaid.[7] They had come to a unity which designated itself as the "house of Judah." The meager evidence gleaned from much later sources would seem to indicate that in this area there was no neat line between Hebrew and non-Hebrew. The "house of Judah" contained Kenite and Midianite and other elements. It finally emerged as an historical unity in the period immediately preceding Saul and David only after a long process involving shifting, settling, and amalgamation by clans and tribes.[8]

At Hebron tradition particularly remembered Abraham, a legendary figure from Mesopotamia who had, the stories said, settled there after wandering around the Fertile Crescent. In this tradition Abraham probably represented the settlement of the Hebron area by Amorite peoples as far back as the nineteenth or eighteenth centuries B.C. To this earliest traceable settlement of the Hebron area other immigrations had been added through the course of the years, and each additional influx of people brought to Hebron new traditions. Of particular importance were traditions which had apparently originated at Kadesh-barnea, an oasis somewhere in the desert to the south of Palestine proper. It may very well be that Kadesh (Mount Sinai was probably in its vicinity[9]) was the original home of the religion and worship of Yahweh. Although the present form of the Pentateuch does not make it too clear because the narrative proper has been obscured by the insertion of several complexes of laws, it was undoubtedly to Kadesh that the Hebrews who had been detained in Egypt fled. Indeed, the repeated word of Moses to Pharaoh, "Let my people go three days journey into the wilderness to serve Yahweh their God," would seem to indicate that the very purpose of their desire to leave Egypt had been to fulfill some obligation to Yahweh at his sanctuary at Kadesh. It may be that this observance was the Passover feast in its original form and that this is why the Passover has become the remembrance par excellence of the deliverance from Egypt.

At any rate, through the arrival in the Hebron area of peoples from Kadesh, the traditions of Yahweh, of his power and righteousness—particularly of the manifestation of his power and righteousness in the deliverance of a band of his people from a situation of hopeless oppression in Egypt—came to Palestine proper. Furthermore, either through the gradual movement northward of the Levitical priests, devotees of Yahweh who had originated at Kadesh, or through the arrival in central Palestine of groups who had come in contact with the traditions of Kadesh before they moved northward on the east side of the Jordan and then westward across it, the figure of Moses and the wonderful story of the escape from Egypt came also to be associated with the traditions of the tribal confederation centered at Shechem or Shiloh.[10]

Thus, what was happening in the land of Palestine between 2000 and 1000 B.C. could be characterized as a conquest by infiltration. The numerous stages and the variety of elements involved in this are indicated by the variety of names appearing as designations of the inhabitants of the land in the shadowy period before the kingdom emerged under Saul and David: Amorites, Canaanites, Hittites, and Horites in the remoter past; Midianites, Calebites, Kenites, Benjamites and the "house of Joseph" in the more immediate past; and, finally, in the period just preceding 1000 B.C., the two great groups centering at Shechem or Shiloh and at Hebron, the tribal confederation of the "sons of Israel" and the amalgamation known as the "house of Judah." [11]

Thus the "people" who became a kingdom in the days of Saul and David had not come into being full-blown. Behind this people lay the kind of complexity and diversity always characteristic of historical entities. Various elements had settled the land at various times. Different groups and different places had different traditions and backgrounds. The sagas of the wandering patriarchs guided by their gods, the stirring accounts of the conquest of places and peoples by heroes such as Joshua and the ancient judges, the vague remembrance of homeless days in the desert that had been wonderfully superseded by the finding of a land where roots could be put down, the awesome awareness of obligation to a god who had manifested himself in the thunders, lightnings, and quakings of the holy mountain whereon he was wont to dwell, the remembrance of deliverance from hopelessness and bondage by the God who spoke through Moses—all these were part of the heritage of the people inhabiting Palestine about 1000 B.C. As this people had, through the years, been formed of various elements, the various traditions had come to be more widely appropriated and more related to one another.

Still, this people was not an organized entity. Apparently the two major divisions, the sons of Israel and the house of Judah, were quite independent of one another. Furthermore, the unity that prevailed inside each major division—and particularly in the case of the sons of Israel—was a loose unity, the unity of a confederation of tribes rather than of a nation with a central government. Indeed, there seems to have been real resistance in the northern confederation to any authority too centralized. It may very well be, for example, that the shift of the sanctuary of the confederation of the sons of Israel from Shechem to Shiloh was occasioned by the attempt of a certain Abimelech to organize the tribes into a monarchy with the capital at Shechem.[12] There was a resistance to anything at all approaching centralization of authority. Even more, for the Yahweh devotees of the northern confederation any approach to kingship in the sense that kingship was found among neighboring peoples was a betrayal of Israel's covenant obligation to Yahweh.

BEHIND THE NARRATIVE: THE RISE OF THE MONARCHY

Between 1200 and 1000 B.C. history took a turn that forced the Hebrews into a radically different organization of themselves. It was in this period that the Philistines—who, through the Greek geographers, gave their own name to Palestine—appeared. The Philistines were part of a southward movement of "sea peoples" from Greece. Having failed in their attempt to establish themselves in Egypt, they landed on the southern coast of Palestine in the fertile land of the coastal plain and established a league of five cities. Like the Hebrews before them, they seem to have merged with the peoples already resident in their territory and to have adopted Semitic names and gods.

From the very beginning the Philistines constituted a major threat to the other inhabitants of Palestine. They were apparently a people large of stature and fierce in battle. After gaining a monopoly in iron, they would not allow the other inhabitants of the land access to that metal for weapons.[13] They controlled the coastal trade routes. All in all, the reputation they achieved terrified their neighbors. And in the twelfth century B.C. they began a relentless push into the inland territory of Palestine, into the home territory of the sons of Israel and the house of Judah.

The sons of Israel in the north central part of Palestine suffered the heaviest Philistine blows. The old independent spirit of the tribal confederation, it became more and more apparent, could provide no adequate basis for the organized, all-out effort needed to stop the Philistines. Finally, although the Old Testament does not directly say so and only alludes to the disaster, Shiloh, the center of the confederation of the sons of Israel, was destroyed, and the sacred ark, the symbol of Yahweh's presence among his tribes, was taken by the Philistines into their own territory.[14] In effect, the Philistines conquered the Hebrews, who now became a subject people.

In the past, in such circumstances, leaders had arisen—had been, as the book of Judges puts it, "raised up by God's spirit" —to rally the tribes of Israel and to throw off the oppression. Such a leader now appeared in the person of Saul of the tribe of Benjamin.[15] The extent of the Philistine domination, however, was such that more was demanded by way of resistance than the spontaneous rallying of earlier days. Israel was forced to move in a direction that was new for her, and she now acclaimed as king the "judge" whom God had raised up. The dire circumstances of Philistine oppression also forced the sons of Israel and the house of Judah into a closer unity. Saul was recognized as king by the latter as well as the former. The Hebrews were now one people in a sense they had never been before. In such a new state they fought a running war with the Philistines for a score of years.[16]

But the transition from free, loose, tribal confederacy (really two such confederacies) to this new state was not an easy one. What outward circumstances had forced upon the Hebrews was not so easily taken up into the fabric of their life. Thus Saul found himself fighting not only against the Philistines but also against tensions threatening to disrupt the unity which the Hebrew tribes had found under him. He apparently came fairly soon into conflict with the priests of the old northern confederation.[17] Their resistance to the new monarchy sprang from the conservatism so often characteristic of religion as well as from the threat that a king posed to their status. The opposition of the priests, however, probably only mirrored more widespread resentment of the new situation.

Saul himself was a product of the older confederation, sensitive to, and appreciative of, its faith and way of life. He held back from making a thoroughgoing reorganization of the monarchy, and this inevitably made him less efficient as king. And this weakness of Saul accounts for the rise of David and for the friction which existed between the two. The conflict and tension between his attachment to the older Israel and the demands made upon his position by the Philistine threat resulted in Saul's apparent mental imbalance.[18] When Saul finally met a hero's death on the battlefield, the Philistine domination was just as strong as it had been at the beginning of his reign.

The Hebrews were threatened, however, not only by the enemy without but also by the tensions within the body politic which Saul's tragic conflict had mirrored. And although they were still resisting any move toward becoming like the nations round about them, yet, given the situation in 1000 B.C., they had come too far on the road of kingship to go back.

It was in the person of David that history at that moment found her man. He was sensitive to what the sons of Israel and the house of Judah had been and held dear, sensitive to these things in such a way that it is hard to draw the line between the point at which he is realistically preserving these things in new situations and the point at which he is merely using them to enhance his own position. Unlike Saul, he was a consummately skillful politician who was able to bring the various elements of the sons of Israel and the house of Judah together in a working coalition, as well as a strategist who knew how to wage war at every military and diplomatic level.

He was a winsome man, with a humanity that can be seen in his sins of passion and, on the positive side, in the attraction he held for the masses of the people and in the loyalty with which he was served by those around him.

David did not immediately move to take over the kingdom of Saul in a way that would appear presumptuous. He mourned Saul's death with obvious sincerity and also with obvious political acumen. He allowed the admirers of Saul to retreat from the Philistines to the east side of the Jordan, there to set up an unstable little kingdom with Saul's son at its head.[19] He made the most of the alliance he had sealed with the Philistines in the days of his flight from the wrath of Saul, and probably allowed them to consider him their vassal until his power had reached the point where they could not withstand it. He consolidated the kingship given him at Saul's death by the house of Judah. Then, when it became clear to the sons of Israel to the north that they must choose between strong leadership (which the remnants of the house of Saul could not provide) and extinction at the hands of the Philistines, David received the elders of the old northern confederation at Hebron and accepted their recognition of him as king. The subjects of Saul were now the subjects of David; and history and David together had conspired to make the position of the second king infinitely more secure than the first king's had been.[20]

David did not, however, stop there. Despite the fact that the sons of Israel and the house of Judah together occupied most of the area of Palestine, there were still places, particularly cities, which they had not taken. Such a city, strategically located and possessing an ancient non-Hebrew religious and cultural tradition, was Jerusalem. David's next move was to capture that city. It is commonly pointed out that since this was a city not formerly associated in any way with either the sons of Israel or the house of Judah, David was providing himself with a neutral center from which he could extend his kingship without involving his royal city in internecine disputes. It is also commonly pointed out that Jerusalem was exceedingly well-located from the military point of view and that, in taking it as his capital, David was providing himself and his successors with such a secure headquarters that, later, the might of Assyria could not capture it and only a long siege brought about its fall to Babylon. There is, however, much more to it than that.

David's problem—and he understood it as Saul had not—was to integrate the ideals of the old Israelite confederation (apparently larger in numbers and stronger in conviction than the house of Judah) with the fact of kingship made necessary by history. The more profound significance of his capture of Jerusalem is related to this problem. From the meager hints available it would appear that before it was taken by David, Jerusalem had been a city-kingdom with a "sacral kingship" cult and theology through which her political, economic, and everyday life were related to the divine. The king was the priest through whom the people approached the gods and through whom the gods showed their favor or disfavor toward the people. David apparently took over this theology and the cult that was associated with it, and "baptized" them so that they became the vehicles through which the religion and worship of Yahweh could find expression in the new kind of situation in which Israel and Judah found themselves.[21]

Moreover, David integrated these new institutions with the older ones. For example, he brought to Jerusalem the ark, the sacred symbol of the sons of Israel, which had been without a permanent resting place since the destruction of Shiloh by the Philistines. David's establishing it in Jerusalem made of that city what Shechem, and later Shiloh, had been: the central sanctuary of the sons of Israel. Since David's move from Hebron to Jerusalem had already brought the center of the house of Judah there, the two premonarchical tribal confederations were now unified in terms of the site which was their center and in the person of David whom each had chosen as king. Furthermore, the kingship theology and cult of Jerusalem, into which the faith and ideals of the various elements of the new unified Israel were focused and through which they now found expression, provided a means for preserving the older traditions in a form that fitted the new situation. Thus David sought—and successfully for at least two generations— to avoid the tension between the old and the new that had destroyed Saul and his kingdom.

All this accomplished, David extended his rule to include other peoples than those who had been the sons of Israel and the house of Judah. The extent of the territory brought under his control as well as the nature of his accomplishment in creating an empire of diverse peoples and territories can be seen in an imaginary reconstruction of the greeting with which David might have been hailed when, on some occasion of state, he appeared in "the city of David." About him would be gathered his troops: his personal, hand-picked corps of elite fighters, the "three" and the "thirty";[22] the people of Israel, the militia of the old northern confederation; the army of the house of Judah; and the foreign mercenaries such as Ittai the Gittite and Uriah the Hittite. Then might have come the acclamation: "David: King of the House of Judah; Covenanted King of the House of Israel; Leader of the Hosts of Yahweh, God of Israel; Successor to Melchizedek as Priest-King of Jerusalem; King of all the cities of the Canaanites; King of Edom; King of Ammon; Overlord of Moab; Emperor of the Provinces of Syria." It was a far cry from the simple court of Saul at Benjamite Gibeah only some twenty years earlier, and it was a much farther cry from what the clans and tribes comprised of the sons of Israel and the house of Judah had been only half a century before.[23]

What David had created was consolidated by his successor Solomon. Jerusalem was made worthy of her place as the chief city of such an empire by the erection of a palace and additional fortifications. From Elath on the Gulf of Akaba to

Megiddo on the plain of Esdraelon, structures of all kinds bespoke the wealth and power of the Hebrew empire. A court of wise men and scribes came into being. Emissaries of foreign powers came and went. And the religious side of David's remarkable unification of the Hebrews found expression in the erection of the Temple, in which Judah's ancient veneration of Yahweh was continued, and the ark of the sons of Israel was enshrined; and there the cult and mythology of the ancient religion of Jerusalem provided a vehicle through which the worship of Yahweh could be adequately offered under the new condition in which the Hebrews found themselves.[24]

BEHIND THE NARRATIVE:
THE EARLIER ACCOUNTS
OF THE MONARCHY

The chief purpose of this chapter is not to reconstruct the history of Israel. It is to say something about the narrative of the Old Testament, particularly the nucleus of that narrative as it is found in the stratum known as the J document, and of the situation which gave rise to its writing. It is, however, only against the kind of background that has been sketched that the full grandeur of the narrative of the Old Testament can be appreciated. The point is that it was the emergence of united Israel as a kingdom under David that prompted the national self-consciousness that resulted in an Israelite literature. And it was the leisure and culture of the royal court, particularly in the time of Solomon and afterward, that made it possible for a national history to be written down. Again it should be emphasized that it is as a national epic that the Old Testament took its origin, not as a religious book in the usual sense of the word. It is the character of that national epic that sets the Old Testament narrative apart from literatures of its own and later times, and lends to it its unique character.

To say that the national history of the united kingdom as

we have it in the Old Testament is unique is not to say that it has nothing of a nationalistic character about it. Indeed, probably the first attempts to write any connected account of the rise of the Israelite monarchy were extremely nationalistic. The question, expressed or implicit, that gives rise to the recounting of any nation's history is: "What does the existence of this nation on the stage of history mean?" The simplest answer to that question is that the continued existence and successful expansion of that nation makes self-evident its worth and worthiness; and the nation itself and its ruling class are to be viewed with uncritical adulation.

Something like that seems to be characteristic of the earliest continuous narratives of the Old Testament.[25] Though the present composite nature of the narrative portions of the Old Testament make absolutely verifiable theories impossible, it is extremely likely that the first attempts to deal with the question of the meaning of the existence of the united monarchy were adulatory of the nation and of its king. Their preoccupation with the wonder of the kingdom that had come into existence, with the success of its attempts to hold back the Philistines, with the way in which the divine favor toward the king had resulted in prosperity and success for the nation, made those attempts shortsighted so far as any real dealing with the history of the kingdom of Saul and David is concerned.

The chief concern of these early narratives was to show how it was the kingdom—and the king who had made it what it was—that saved Israel and Judah from the chaos which had characterized the days immediately before the rise of Saul; that halted the Philistine advance with its threat to the very existence of the Hebrew people; and that put Israel and Judah "on the map" of the ancient Near East. Their main concern, quite unlike the modern one which separates the sacred from the secular, was to show that the success of the kingdom and its king was the sign both of the power of Yahweh to have his way in the world and of the favor of Yahweh toward his people.

The Witness of the Narrative   27

So it is that the earlier narrative underlying the books of Samuel emphasizes the divine initiative in the rise of Saul to kingship.[26] It makes the point that it was the action of Yahweh himself that brought the kingdom into being. In the days of the writing of this narrative, however, it was not the house of Saul that had come to be the royal house of the united monarchy but the house of David. The narrative of which we are speaking makes it clear, therefore, that Saul was beset with a basic weakness which made his rejection and fall inevitable. The view that it was really David who was Yahweh's man is made apparent, and the greatness of the founder of the royal house is proclaimed in romantic hero legends. Once a man of the stature of David has entered the stage, the Philistines fall back before him; Jerusalem comes readily into his hands, the Ammonites, Moabites, Edomites, and the rest of the neighbors of Israel come under his rule. Indeed, the theme of this narrative, probably originating in the reign of David himself, is tersely put in II Samuel 8:15: "So David reigned over all Israel; and David administered justice and equity to all his people."

Yet, even in its earliest forms, the narrative literature in which the rise of the united Israelite monarchy is celebrated never completely compromises the truth to the glorification of the king and the kingdom. Though the fact that Saul had been the first king must have been of considerable embarrassment and inconvenience to the house of David, both because of the personal popularity of Saul and because of the fact he continued to be representative of the old premonarchical days, nonetheless the greatness of Saul shines through the narrative. Saul's divine choice is emphasized, his heroism is made clear, and the narrative shows how, even in the days of his failure and mental derangement, David could not supplant him and had to flee him even in David's own home territory.

All this is to say that the narrators had an interest in history that could not be overridden either by nationalism or by their desire to glorify the house of David. There was a consciousness that even a divinely appointed king was human and, like all men, stood under the rule of God. Indeed, the account of the complications at court which led to the succession of Solomon to David's throne (II Samuel 9-20, and I Kings 1-2)—an account probably independent in origin—is one of the most remarkably frank and straightforward pieces of writing in all antiquity.[27]

The writer of this acocunt recognizes the greatness and astuteness of David, is aware of the sway of David over men and of his ability to bring and hold diverse elements into a kingdom. With unrelenting and uncompromising discernment, however, the author sees the flaw in David's character which more than once led the kingdom to the brink of disintegration. From the infatuation with Bath-sheba to which the conduct of war had to play second fiddle, through the indulgence of his children that led to Absalom's revolt, to the intrigue of a conniving court prophet and a favorite wife to secure the succession for Solomon, the inside story of the reign of David is told without moralism but with such appreciation of the subtle interplay of cause and effect in the matrix of human history as to make this narrative great literature. There is a concern here for truthful reporting of the events of history which is not intimidated by the power or success of the house of David. More than that, there is a concern for the truth in terms of the total course that history is taking. It was out of this concern, and not out of the desire to make some specifically religious point, that the really great epic of ancient Israel was born.

THE BASIS OF THE NARRATIVE:
THE J DOCUMENT[28]

Either sometime during the reign of Solomon when the course of events began to tarnish the overly idealistic views of the monarchy, or after his death when the split of the monarchy into two kingdoms gave the lie to any view of history built only on the success of David, the J Document or the Yahwist Epic, which is the basic nucleus of the narrative parts of the Old Testament, was written.[29] And it was in this J Document that the question of the place of the united kingdom on the larger stage of history, in so far as that stage was known to an Israelite of the tenth century B.C., was raised and answered in terms of history itself.

It is not entirely anachronistic to say that in the way he went about answering his question, the J writer was a working historian, utilizing the sources available to him. He did not, of course, treat his material in the way that a post-seventeenth-century critical historian does. His finished work was much more a simple putting together of his sources than a modern historical work would be His concern, however, was more like the concern of a Toynbee than the concern of a "religious" writer. His aim was to trace the course of events out of which the united Israel of his day had arisen and, in terms of the course of these events, to determine what gave meaning to the flow of history.[30]

The most obvious materials available to the J writer were, of course, those early narratives in which the rise of the monarchy had been recounted and the course of events up to the time of Solomon had been traced.[31] The J writer, however, was no time-bound provincial Israelite for whom history was defined simply by what his grandfather could remember. He recognized that the historical forces that had converged to produce the empire of David and Solomon did not begin with the Philistine threat and the rise of Saul; he was aware that the roots of the present lay in a more remote past.

Now three points must be borne in mind in connection with the probing of the past that resulted in the J writer's narrative. The first is that once he got behind the immediate past, the J writer was not dealing with one nation, nor with any simple unity. There was, that is to say, no unified national story which he had simply to commit to writing. Once he got back more than one, or at the most two, generations, he was dealing with the two great entities, the sons of Israel and the house of Judah, and with the diverse clans, tribes, traditions, and waves of immigration which had gone into the formation of those entities. Although the way in which history had gradually brought these various elements together had undoubtedly resulted in a certain amount of unification of traditions, the J writer had to discover for himself some point of view or some principle of interpretation that would connect events to form one story.

The second point is that the J writer was, it is universally agreed, a southerner. His own native traditions were those of the house of Judah, and what he knew of the traditions and point of view of the sons of Israel, he knew from the outside. This is seen in the obvious priority given by the J writer to Abraham, the patriarch of Hebron, as well as in many other ways. Furthermore, he was obviously an enthusiast, albeit a realistic one, with regard to the Davidic empire. For him it was the present climax of the history that lay behind it; it was that to which things had been leading. Yet his own southern origins and his own enthusiasm for the Davidic empire did not result in his ignoring the traditions of the sons of Israel. Indeed, one of his principal aims seems to have been to show that the course of history had led to a unity that was more basic than the monarchy itself or the house of David.

The third point is that the J writer did not invent *de novo* the point of view from which he looked back at history nor the way of putting things together in a connected story. It was his conviction that it was in the God Yahweh the course of history had meaning. This conviction was not new with him. It is expressed in what is probably an ancient *credo* in Deuteronomy 26:5-9; it was certainly implied in the faith of the old confederation of the sons of Israel; and it may very well have been already behind an earlier southern attempt to trace the history behind the kingdom, an attempt which the J writer utilized and expanded.[32] It was, nevertheless, the J writer who put this conviction to work in a significant way as the interpretative principle by which history could be explained.

So it was that the J writer looked beyond the immediate stories of the rise of the monarchy and of the glory of David and his house to see what more profound and thorough historical explanation could be found for the existence of the united monarchy. He discovered the heart of what he was seeking in the great event of some two or three centuries before, in which Israel, through the discernment and interpretation of Moses, had become conscious of the significance of her existence as a people. Thus, the core of the J Document, as of the entire completed Pentateuch, is the account of the exodus from Egypt.

What did the J writer, and the tradition that lay behind him, say about the exodus? It was his basic contention that through that event Yahweh had acted to reveal himself as the one whose power was such that only his purpose could prevail in human history. This was the meaning of the escape of a group of powerless, hopeless nomads from the might of Egypt. Yahweh had acted in such a way as to "let in," to disclose to, those participating in the exodus, who he was, and the graciousness and righteousness of his purpose. For J the primary importance of Moses was that he had seen that this was so and had interpreted to Israel the exodus for what it really was. Israel, J was saying as Moses had said, is to be defined as the people who remember the exodus. As such, the primary significance of their existence as a people is to be found in their knowledge of Yahweh, of his power and righteousness, and of the fact of his sovereignty over history. The real significance of the emergence of Israel as a nation in the united monarchy is that the people who possess the clue to the meaning of human history have attained a place in history from which they can act and speak effectively. The real significance of the existence of

Israel is that they are the people who know *who* is God. And the purpose of their existence is to bear witness to the fact that Yahweh is God.

Thus in the story of the exodus, undoubtedly elaborated as it had been handed down through the years before his own time, the J writer discerned the clue to the meaning of the events that had led to the Davidic empire. And in terms of what that event had come to mean in the faith of Israel the J writer found the thread of meaning that held all the other events of history together. Once faith had discerned the presence of Yahweh in the great exodus event, once in that event the character of Yahweh had been revealed, then the J writer saw that the sovereign purpose of Yahweh provided the clue to the meaning of all history.

So it was that the J writer could put together in a narrative that moved in a connected way from creation to the monarchy all the disparate and various traditions, wanderings, conquests, and settlements that lay behind the emergence of the sons of Israel and the house of Judah as historical entities. Although the analysis of a pure "historicism" might show how the traditions of Abraham reflected an Amorite settlement of Hebron which was not really connected with the settlement of central Palestine reflected in the traditions of Jacob, the J writer had raised the question of the over-all meaning of history, and saw these and innumerable other traditions all as elements in the great historical process which had led to the existence of a kingdom with security, territory, and a culture through all of which the fact of Yahweh's sovereignty over history could be proclaimed.

Such a faith—or philosophy of history—is the background against which the J writer recounted the steps that had led to the kingdom. He began with the traditions that went farthest back, that already had taken root in places such as Hebron, Beer-sheba, and Beth-el when the more specifically Hebrew peoples entered Palestine. These traditions undoubtedly went back to the period of shifting populations in the Fertile Crescent mirrored in other ancient Near Eastern records. They went back to a period in which there was no extensive domination of the Palestinian area by one great imperial power, when wandering clans dealt only with the kings and princes of small city-kingdoms. They went back to a period in which the pattern of what was to be had not yet become clear.

J, therefore, characterized this period as one of promise. The patriarchal ancestors (this, subsequent history had proved them to be), Abraham and Isaac and Jacob, were on the move. They were confident in the goodness of the purpose of Yahweh for them and for their seed, but they were not aware of what that purpose was to be. Separate though the origins of the groups they represented may have been, and separate though the places may have been where each of them was revered, their movements, their troubles, and their settlings down were, for J, connected in the purpose of Yahweh. J, therefore, tied the traditions of the patriarchs together into a connected narrative, and in doing this, followed undoubtedly a tendency already present in the oral tradition before his own time.

It was, however, only in the miraculous escape of one group of Hebrews from enslavement in Egypt that the nature of Yahweh's purpose began to be laid open. It was in that event that Yahweh, for J, began to be known for what he really was. Then, just as it had been the purpose discerned in the exodus that had tied together the various strands of history preceding it, so it was that purpose which had given a unity to the more recent course of events by which various clans and tribes, and then the two great confederations, had been brought together in the united kingdom. It was in terms of Yahweh and his purpose for the people he was bringing into existence to witness to his sovereignty in history that the traditions of various groups were related to one another by the J writer.

We have seen how the traditions of Shechem, with their emphasis on law and covenant and upon the divine revelation at a desert mountain, had not originally very much to do with the clans and tribes whose premonarchical life centered at Hebron. We have seen also how Kadesh-barnea in the desert south of Palestine figured importantly in the traditions of the people at Hebron, but not in the Shechem traditions. Many other traditions preserved in the Pentateuch undoubtedly originated separately with various groups who entered Palestine at various times and in various places. In the present form of the narrative, however, all these traditions have been related to one another so that the impression is given that Israel was always one people. The impression is given by the J writer that the traditions of the separate groups are related to one another in a chronological sequence as the remembered experience of one united people.

In the way of a Semite of the tenth century B.C., this writer was saying that the course of history, however complex it may be, is held together by the purpose of Yahweh for it. J sees the united Israelite monarchy, which existed in his own time, or which had just separated into two kingdoms, as no accident. He sees that monarchy as no mere tribute to the worthiness or the competence of its royal house. He sees that monarchy as the latest step in the working out of a purpose. That purpose had slowly been revealed in the events that had led up to the monarchy, but most clearly and supremely in the exodus. For J it was that purpose, the purpose of Yahweh God, that made sense of history.

One further point remains to be made: J was not provincial in his view of the events of history. Not only did he write a history that made sense of the united Israelite monarchy in terms of the past history of the various groups that made it up, but he related the history of that people to the history of the whole world as far as it was possible for him to know it in his time. J set Israel's history in the wider context of the current myths of human origins and the prehistory of mankind. Moreover, although it would be wrong to suppose that the J writer held any doctrine of sin as understood in the later sense, he did use the myths of the origin of the world and of man to illustrate the human problem as he saw it. In doing this, he was enunciating what was implied in that Israelite faith upon which he built his history. In these stories from the culture of which he was a part—the stories of creation, of man's expulsion from the garden of paradise, of the first murder, of the great primeval flood, and of the vain attempt of man to rival the gods which resulted in the confusion of human languages—J was making a point which makes him and Israel's faith unique. He was saying that the human problem does not lie in the weakness and uncertainty in which man must face the forces of nature. The human problem is not, primarily, finitude. Certainly, J was saying, man *is* a creature. This, if man would only understand it aright in terms of the goodness and power of the God whose creature he is, is a good thing. It is, however, just here that the problem lies so far as J is concerned. Man has not rightly understood who he is. He has rebelled against his creatureliness and, in so doing, has separated himself from the God whose creature he is. He has created a situation in which things are not right between himself and God. The real problem of human existence is to be right with the God, Yahweh, who made all things and whose purpose gives history its meaning.

And it is in terms of this problem, which is the problem of all men, that the story J has to tell finds its basic meaning. It is in the vague discernment of promise on the part of the legendary patriarchs that Yahweh first begins to work. It is in the great event of the exodus that he reveals himself, the goodness of his purpose and his power, with which the purpose can be brought to accomplishment. And it is in the subsequent history of the settlement of Palestine and the growing unity of the sons of Israel and the house of Judah that has led to the formation of the united monarchy that Yahweh has been creating a people whose existence could be the means by which all peoples could find what their existence means. That is to say that the significance of the history of Israel, the history that has led to the empire of David, is that it is the particular history in which the clue to the meaning of all history is to be found. It is in acknowledgment of the sovereignty of Yahweh, which his dealings with Israel have shown to be good and righteous altogether, that man's life becomes what it was created to be.

There is, then, a theology in the writing of J. The theology that is there, however, does not arise from some narrowly "religious" concern. J, standing at the point where the reality of the united monarchy dominated history for him, raised the question of the meaning of the juncture to which history had come. The answer which he found, as he looked back over the course of history, was a theological answer. But it was theological only because that happened to be the only answer which, for J, could adequately deal with the questions he had raised. The God to whom J and his narrative were bearing witness was not the end-point of some "religious" quest in which the questions were loaded and the conclusions preconceived. The God of whom J and his narrative were speaking had compelled faith in himself in terms of certain events as well as in terms of an over-all history. Without that God neither the events nor the total history of which they were a part could be explained for J.

All this simply says more concretely what was said in the introduction. The religion of the Old Testament is not just religion, but historical religion. And this is true in a double way. First of all, that religion rests upon certain historical events in which faith has discovered God at work revealing himself and his purpose and bringing that purpose to accomplishment. This was certainly the way in which J looked back at everything, particularly the exodus, which had led to the establishment of the great empire of David. Secondly, the religion of the Old Testament is a historical religion in that it is always some present configuration of events that leads to a recognition of the significance of previous events in the purpose of God. This, in the case of J, was true of the monarchy which he knew. It was his question about, or conviction about, the significance of his present under God that led him to say what he did about the past.

Finally, the J writer took history seriously in still another sense. Although he was certain that the explanation of history was to be found in the character and purpose of Yahweh, J did not presume to define the ultimate outcome of the course of history. He left his story open at the end.[33] There is, in the strict sense of the word, no eschatology in J. That is, no prediction is made about just where history is going. Nothing definite, indeed nothing at all, is said of the outcome of things. Yet, the J work is eschatological in a broader sense of the word. The conclusion is an open-ended one. History, complex and living, has led to the Davidic empire. The fullness of the purpose of Yahweh, in which history finds its meaning, is not to be identified with any time or with any person in that history. The *whole sequence* is the area in which Yahweh's purpose has been, and is, working. But the whole thing is not yet finished. History is still going on.

What J has done is to advance a view of history, and to bear witness to a faith in God in terms of which history, after his own time, can be approached. He has made it possible for later men, in whom his own view of things has taken root, to define the meaning of later times in terms of the purpose of God. J has, in a very real sense, begun a story which only the completion of the course of all of history can finish. It is in this sense that he has left to us something more than mere religion. It is in this sense that his narrative bears witness to a God who, if J's witness be true, is alone worthy of the name.

Upon the foundation laid by J others were to build. With this nucleus, the J Document, other strands were to be combined until the narrative found in the books from Genesis through II Kings reached its present form. It was, however, the great J epic, dating from the tenth century B.C., which began the distinctive biblical witness to the God who is some *one* and who is known in terms of the history over which and in which he reigns.

CHAPTER TWO

The Witness of the Law

The Pentateuch by no means contains only narrative. At the point where the Israelites who escaped from Egypt arrive at Mount Sinai, the narrative is interrupted by the giving of the law to Moses. This interruption begins at Exodus 20, runs right through the Book of Leviticus, and continues into the tenth chapter of Numbers. Furthermore, when, later on, the narrative has brought the Israelites to the border of the promised land, there is a pause during which Moses lays down a "second law," Deuteronomy. To account for the narrative, therefore, is by no means to account for the contents of the Pentateuch. Something must also be said about the law and its place in the Old Testament.

Law in the Old Testament cannot, however, be separated from narrative. No separate book of law, entirely outside the context of a narrative, exists. This statement is not violated by Leviticus, for that book never stood alone outside the context of the whole Pentateuch. Even though there are strands in the Old Testament in which law is emphasized, Israel always saw the origin of the law in the context of the events by which she had been called into existence as a people. The law could not be separated from history.

Thus, the principle noted before applies once again. The Old Testament is a book attached firmly to history. This is as true of its legal as of its narrative sections. Moreover, in respect to the law, the connection with history is twofold: Israel remembers the law as having originated in events of long ago, but it is the course of events in some nearer present which prompts some men to organize and set down a record of what originated in the past. This chapter, therefore, will consider first the origins of law in ancient Israel, and then the times and circumstances which prompted the writing of the laws as we find them in the Old Testament.

THE BASIS OF THE LAW: COVENANT

Law comes into existence wherever men live together in society. In some form or other, written or unwritten, it is the basis upon which human relationships are ordered. It grows out of a need. Israel's law has this in common with all law. Furthermore, the particular content of Israel's law undoubtedly has contacts with law in the form in which it was found elsewhere in the ancient Near East. It can be demonstrated that the laws of the Old Testament have affinities with Hurrian, Canaanite, and Babylonian law.[1] There is no doubt that all this is true. To discuss only in such terms, however, the origin of Old Testament law is to miss the main point.

The content, and even the form, of Hebrew law was determined, as we should expect, by the form and content of legal codes in the culture of which the Hebrews were a part. But the real meaning of Hebrew law, its more basic significance, has to be sought along other lines. One of those lines is the situation in the ninth century B.C., which provided the first great impetus to a "scriptural" codification of the law. The other, which will now occupy our attention, is the covenant which figured so importantly in the northern premonarchical tribal confederation of the sons of Israel.

Light on the meaning of covenant has been sought in the covenant contracts prevalent among the nomadic Arabs. There the covenant involves a mutual agreement, entered into by two individuals, by two groups, or by an individual and a group. The effect of the covenant is that peace prevails between the two parties concerned. In the sense that the soul of Jonathan was "knit" to the soul of David, the covenant brings two parties together so that they are one in will and in act. Each in his own way comes to be motivated by the common good. Such a covenant is a contract under which there is mutual obligation, but a contract that is much more than legalistic in nature.[2]

Something of this is undoubtedly true of the covenant between Yahweh and Israel. For example, it is this aspect of it that moves Hosea and Jeremiah to speak in tender and moving terms of the relationship between Yahweh and Israel as one between a lover and the beloved. Yet simply to conceive of the covenant between Yahweh and Israel as one of mutual obligation, even in terms of love instead of law, would be to misunderstand the constraint laid upon Israel by the covenant.

Recent research has shown that the origins of the form of the covenant between Israel and Yahweh are to be sought in a more special type of covenant into which the great Hittite empire entered with subject peoples.[3] This latter type of covenant was really a suzerainty treaty. It was no agreement between equals, but a pact in which the conquered and subject people bound itself to the conqueror. It was a pact in which the sovereignty of the conqueror was acknowledged by the subject.

These Hittite suzerainty treaties took a special form. They did not simply list the obligations of the two parties involved. The Hittite emperor, the conqueror, would first recite the acts that entitled him to the homage about to be pledged by the subject ruler and his people. He would establish his right to such homage by telling of the might of his rule as it had prevailed in his battles and his relations with other nations. When this recital was finished, the obligations owed the Hittite emperor by the subject people would be listed. Thus the regulations were not just arbitrarily laid down: they were the inevitable result of what the Hittite emperor was and had done. They were the description of what it was meet and right for a subject people to be, given the might of the Hittites.

A little reflection by anyone familiar with the Old Testament will immediately make it clear that the form of these Hittite suzerainty treaties is very similar to the form in which the covenant and Israel's obligations under it are set down in the Old Testament. In Joshua 24, for example, where we are told of the covenant made under Joshua at Shechem, there is first a recital of the "mighty acts" of Yahweh through which Israel has come to know him (verses 1-13). In view of this, the obligation to fear and to serve Yahweh is stated, and the choice which Israel must make is outlined (verses 14-18). Finally, in view of what Yahweh has done, Israel acknowledges the debt under which she stands, and pledges humble service to him (verses 19 ff.).

The same basic form underlies Deuteronomy. That book takes the form of a speech delivered by Moses to Israel as they stand in the plains of Moab about to cross the Jordan into Palestine. The outline of the book is just the same as the outline of Joshua 24. First comes a recital of the deeds through which the might and sovereignty of Yahweh have come to be known (basically, chapters 1-11). Then comes a detailed outline of the obligations incumbent upon Israel because of her subjection to and dependence upon Yahweh (chapters 12-26). Finally, Deuteronomy closes with further exhortation and a description of the ceremony in which Israel undertakes her responsibility under the covenant (chapters 27-31). In Deuteronomy each element of the pattern is elaborated more than in Joshua 24, but it is the same pattern and there is no doubt of its affinities with the Hittite suzerainty treaties.

This pattern, which underlies not only Joshua 24 and Deuteronomy but other legal sections of the Old Testament as well, undoubtedly originated—in the case of the Hebrews—in the north. And scholars have come to see it as an important element in the life of the old tribal confederation of the sons of Israel, first at Shechem and then at Shiloh. In point of fact, it is with Shechem that both Joshua 24 and Deuteronomy 27 associate the covenant ceremony.[4]

The cult of the covenant, however, may go back further than specifically Israelite settlement at Shechem, back further than the worship there of Yahweh. Just a few hints that Shechem was originally the site of worship of "El berith" or "Baal berith" are left (Judges 9:46; 8:33; 9:4). These names mean "god of the covenant" or "lord of the covenant," and the way in which they are used in Judges indicates that these deities were non-Israelite. Since it is not likely that a new god came to be acknowledged at Shechem after the Israelites had taken it over, it is reasonable to suppose that this was the name of the deity anciently associated with the sanctuary there. The incorporation of the covenant concept into the worship of Yahweh at Shechem by the Israelites after their arrival would be one more instance of that tendency toward unification which was operative all through the history of ancient Israel and which furnished the guiding principle by which the J writer organized the history leading up to the united monarchy.[5]

Thus, probably before specifically Israelite settlement at Shechem, there was a cult there the expressed pattern of which had somehow been influenced by the form of the Hittite suzerainty treaties. It is undoubtedly from this cult that there came many of the details of the legend of the theophany of God in thunder and lightning at the giving of the law. It is probably out of the fusion of older Israelite traditions with the traditions of pre-Israelite Shechem that there also came the confusion over the name of the mountain on which the law was given. The traditions of the south—J and the Priestly Code—always call the mountain "Sinai," while the northern tradition—the

E Document, Deuteronomy, and the Elijah stories—always call it "Horeb."

At some point, probably some three or four centuries before the time of Saul and David, the "gospel" of the God Yahweh who had delivered a helpless and hopelessly oppressed people from the power of Egypt was brought to Shechem. This may have been, as we have seen, the result of the arrival of peoples who had journeyed northward from Kadesh-barnea on the east side of the Jordan and then crossed westward into Palestine. More likely, it was the result of the arrival at Shechem of members of the priestly tribe or caste of Levi, the particularly devoted adherents of Yahweh who ultimately gained control of the shrine at Shechem.[6]

However it happened, Shechem became Yahweh's sanctuary, and the traditions of Shechem came to be associated with Yahweh. In the same way that expanding Christianity "baptized" and made use of Greek philosophy as well as local cults and customs and legends in Europe, the cult of the covenant and the legend associated with it were used to express the obligation under which the devotees of Yahweh stood to their God. Furthermore, it is easy to see how Moses, who had been so instrumental in interpreting the meaning of the great exodus event to those who had experienced it, would come to be associated with the traditions and legends of the cult of the covenant at Shechem when the covenant became the expression of the obligation to Yahweh laid upon Israel by the exodus.

The sanctuary at Shechem and the cult associated with it were the chief means by which the confederation of tribes occupying the territory in the northern and north central part of Palestine were held together. The corporate memory of these groups was not so short that they were unable to remember the austerity and precariousness of life in the desert. Each of them had had the experience of occupying or winning by conquest footholds in Palestine which, though not one of the most fertile areas of the world, looked to desert nomads like "a land flowing with milk and honey." Bound together as they were by a common memory and a common experience of finding a homeland, they came to be more explicitly bound together in the covenant of Yahweh. They came to regard the destiny which had brought them together by comparatively similar paths as no accident, but as the result of the sway over history of the God who had led his people safely out of the clutches of Egyptian power and bound them to him in the covenant.

Hard put as the members of the confederation of the sons of Israel were to maintain the footholds they had gained in Palestine, it is easy to see how this conviction of a destiny presided over by Yahweh led them to regard the battles by which they retained and expanded their holdings not as their own, but as "holy wars" of Yahweh. It is also easy to see how one of the most important features of their loosely knit association was the obligation of each of the member clans or tribes to come to the aid of the others when something threatened that destiny in Palestine which they believed to be the purpose of Yahweh for them. The song of Deborah in Judges 5 is an ancient war song of the confederation which illustrates how Yahweh was believed to have come from his desert home to the south to fight for his people and how the various members of the confederation had been summoned to fight for him.[7]

It can also be understood how the foreign culture of the Canaanite city-kingdoms in northern and north central Palestine came to be despised by the devotees of Yahweh there. The resistance of these city-kingdoms to the sons of Israel resulted not only in Israelite contempt for their institutions and religions, but also in the conviction that the ways of the Canaanites were abhorrent to Yahweh. Particularly was this true of kingship which, in the city-kingdoms, always had about it non-Israelite sacral aspects.[8] Thus kingship, as it existed in the cities of Canaan, was something by which the sons of Israel would not be governed. Their God, the God whose might had led them from a nomadic existence in the desert to this promised land, was a God to whom they were obligated under a covenant more like a suzerainty treaty than a merely religious rule. It would be an affront to him for the sons of Israel to subject themselves to a king. Kingship in Israel would be a denial of his exclusive sovereignty. We have already mentioned how just such a breach of the covenant by the inhabitants of Shechem may have been the cause of the moving of the central sanctuary of the confederation to Shiloh.

All this explains how the heroes of the days preceding the monarchy came to be called "judges." The primary claim of each of the judges to eminence in Israel is the loyalty and bravery with which, in some time of threat or danger, he arose to carry forward that conquering purpose of Yahweh of which the settlement of Palestine by the sons of Israel was a part. It was his exemplary demonstration of the covenant demand of exclusive loyalty to Yahweh as lord that gave him the right to "judge" under the covenant—to define, in terms of the implications of the covenant, what was "legal" in any given situation. But his authority, by virtue of which, like Deborah, he might sit under a sacred tree and give judgment (Judges 4:5), did not inhere in himself or in some formal office; nor could it be passed on hereditarily. The authority of the judge was the authority of the covenant to which the judge had been exceptionally loyal. The authority of the judge resulted from the coming to him of the "spirit of Yahweh." [9] Authority, so far as the sons of Israel were concerned, found its source only in Yahweh, the lord of the covenant. Only by his rule, by his covenant, could the law which ordered life be defined.

THE COVENANT TRADITION
UNDER THE KINGDOM

When Philistine expansion made clear the need for closely organized rule such as a king could give, those elements in the monarchy whose roots and heritage lay in the old confederation of the sons of Israel were reluctant to go all the way down the road to kingship. They—and particularly their priests who had been most intimately involved in the older way of life—resisted the steps that Saul had to take as king. After Saul was slain in battle and his son's weak kingdom collapsed, they went to Hebron and recognized David as king; but they did this only after he "had made a covenant with them in Hebron before Yahweh" (II Samuel 5:3). It is not unreasonable to suppose that behind those words lies an agreement which the leaders of the sons of Israel demanded of David that the obligations of Israel under covenant with Yahweh be honored. Only on such a condition would they anoint him king. David might capture Jerusalem and take over the cult of that city with its emphasis on the king as leader of the people and the instrument through which the god showed favor or disfavor, but he could not keep within his kingdom the sons of Israel if his kingship became so pretentious that it did not bow before the covenant obligation to Yahweh under which Israel stood.

Apparently certain elements of the sons of Israel were restive even under David. For Absalom, in preparing the ground for his revolt, appealed to their attachment to the older way of life (II Samuel 15:1-6); and a certain Sheba based his revolt against David on the claim that members of "Israel" had "no portion in David" (II Samuel 20:1).

After David's death we hear nothing of Solomon renewing the covenant between the sons of Israel and the kingdom. Whether this is due to a lacuna in the narrative or to the fact that Solomon considered his office hereditary and felt himself so secure as not to be questioned, we do not know. Under Solomon, however, there was unrest in the north, the leader of which was that Jeroboam who was to become the first northern king after Solomon's death (I Kings 11:26-40). All this destroys any preconceptions we might have of all Israel as one entity and shows that the sons of Israel were never unmindful of their own identity or of the demand of the covenant for exclusive loyalty to Yahweh. Recognition of a king was always for them ambiguous and compromising.

Solomon's successor on the throne of David was Rehoboam. David had come all the way from leadership of a band of outlawed brigands living off the land in the hills of Judah to the kingship, and the empire that Solomon inherited was David's personal achievement. With Rehoboam, however, the third generation of the Davidic dynasty reached its majority, a generation that had known nothing but life in the royal court at Jerusalem. Rehoboam would not have been aware of the background of the various elements of which his empire was composed. He would have considered himself the rightful, hereditary successor to all that had been David's and Solomon's.

Such, however, was not the prevalent attitude in that part of the Davidic empire composed of the sons of Israel and their descendants. To them the covenant that had bound the tribes together under Yahweh was more ancient and more binding than the covenant made with David at Hebron. Not only were the circumstances of Philistine aggression that had made the latter agreement necessary now past, but that agreement had not, in the first place, been binding with regard to the descendants of David. Under Solomon the kingdom of David had become indistinguishable from the kingdoms round about it. The sacred ark of the old confederation might rest in the temple at Jerusalem, but that temple and the cult carried on there proclaimed the glory of the house of David more than the absolute sway of Yahweh. The time had come, from the point of view of the sons of Israel, for a reassessment of relations.

All this lay behind Rehoboam's meeting with the "assembly of Israel" at Shechem which resulted in the separation of the tribes of the north from the Davidic kingdom (I Kings 12). We must allow for the fact that the records we have come to us through the descendants of those who remained loyal to the house of David.[10] This is why the account of the meeting at

Shechem describes the complaints of the northern tribes simply as having to do with taxation and the labor levy, and not with the more significant questions of what the ancient covenant implied. This is why the narrative as it stands takes the position that the separation of the north from the south was rebellion.

Such, however, was not the position of the north. The sons of Israel, were, in their own point of view, independent of any hereditary claim of the house of David, and free to recognize or not to recognize each successor of David on whatever terms they might choose. Their understanding of the situation was at complete odds with that of Rehoboam. On his part, the king would not even grant their right to protest. The sons of Israel, therefore, departed shouting—this time to permanent effect—the cry sounded at the abortive uprising of Sheba half a century or so before:

> What portion have we in David?
>   We have no inheritance in the son of Jesse.
> To your tents, O Israel!
>   Look now to your own house, David. (I Kings 12:16)

Thus, after almost a century together, the sons of Israel and the house of Judah were now (about 920 B.C.) once again separate entities. So effectively, however, had their separate traditions been welded together during that century—due in no small measure to the work of the J writer—that the house of Judah, now the kingdom of David in Jerusalem, could consider itself the true Israel. But from the point of view of those who separated themselves from Rehoboam, only the descendants of the sons of Israel in the north were the true Israel, and this in spite of the fact that the ark remained in Jerusalem. From their point of view, as we have seen, the sons of Israel had simply withdrawn the recognition they had been giving the Davidic monarchy.

The passage of time, however, had made it impossible any

longer for the northern tribes to govern themselves in the manner of the old confederation. A century had passed since the days when the sons of Israel moved about among the Canaanite cities in the fashion of gypsies. They now held those cities, and they were now the established people of the land. Economically, politically, and militarily they could no longer live under the older, simpler polity. And if they were now to exist independently of the kingdom of David, the sons of Israel had now themselves to become a kingdom.

And this they did under Jeroboam, the son of Nebat who, as a leader of dissident northern elements in the time of Solomon, had been exiled to Egypt. Although the stories of the association of Ahijah the prophet with Jeroboam must contain a legendary element, they nevertheless do indicate that even the more radical supporters of the ancient way of life in the north recognized that they could never successfully separate from the kingdom of David and maintain themselves without having a leader of their own in place of the Davidic monarch (I Kings 11 and 12).

From the start Jeroboam faced a contradiction that was not only to weaken his position but to plague his successors. This contradiction was that the most enthusiastic supporters of separation from the Davidic kingdom, those who had brought him to power, were by conviction strongly opposed to absolutist monarchy. Thus, any attempt he or his successors made to strengthen the position of their kingship was opposed by the very elements which supported them against the Davidic kingdom. The *raison d'être* of the northern kingdom was the covenant loyalty to Yahweh, a loyalty that precluded the kind of enthusiasm for the kingdom that alone could make it strong. This was why, even though the territory of the northern kingdom was more extensive than that of the southern kingdom—and wealthier—its first forty-six years of existence saw three dynasties rise and fall, and three of the five kings meet violent deaths. Of course, other factors contributed to this instability. The basic cause, however, lay in what the sons of Israel had been before the Davidic kingdom.[11]

In 876 B.C., after one king had been assassinated and his assassin-successor had taken his own life by burning his palace around him, Omri, the leader of the army of the northern kingdom, took matters into his own hands. He became the strongest king ever to reign north of Jerusalem. The account of Omri's reign occupies only eight verses in I Kings, for neither the theology of the editors of that book nor the later view that only the Davidic house had validly ruled could recognize the achievement of Omri. Yet the success of this king's attempt to put an end to the bickering that had weakened the northern kingdom and to make that kingdom a power to be reckoned with is indicated by the fact that the records of the Assyrian empire, long after Omri's death, referred to Palestine as "the land of Omri." [12]

The achievement of Omri in the north parallels that of David in the south. Omri consolidated the power and the territory of the northern kingdom. He chose a site not formerly associated with any segment of that kingdom and made it his capital. Modern excavations have indicated the extent and the grandeur of the building done by the house of Omri at Samaria. "The ivory palaces that he built" were to be remembered as an outstanding feature of the reign of Ahab, Omri's son and successor (I Kings 22:39).[13]

Hints given in the Old Testament together with the evidence of the Assyrian records and of the excavations at Samaria indicate that the house of Omri turned its back on the antiquated traditions of the sons of Israel and set out to make itself the ruling dynasty of a truly powerful monarchy. One definite way Omri showed his break with the tradition of exclusive loyalty to Yahweh was by establishing close relations with the city-kingdom of Tyre, immediately to the north of Palestine. Omri's reason for this alliance with Tyre was probably twofold. First, it was to his advantage to have an ally in this close neighbor, given the pressure from the northeast by the Syrians and Assyrians. Second, Tyre had an ancient, impressive tradition of kingship, from which Omri could profit in his attempt to strengthen his position as king. To further this alliance, Ahab, the son and heir of Omri, was married to Jezebel, the daughter of the king of Tyre.[14]

The aims of Omri, then, and the steps taken to achieve those aims, very closely paralleled the aims and methods of David a century and a quarter before. A capital was established from which the monarchy could operate unencumbered by any unsympathetic local tradition; the territory was expanded and the borders made secure by conquest and alliance; and apparently an attempt was made to connect the monarchy with a religious tradition upon which it could draw for prestige and strength.

In the south, however, the monarchy and the religion of Yahweh had become so firmly wedded that the monarchy and the institutions connected with it became efficient vehicles for expressing loyalty to, and worship of, Yahweh. So much was this the case that the term used to designate the king—*messiah* (anointed)—was later to become the designation of the one expected at the climax of history as inaugurator of the kingdom of God.[15]

But the traditions and history of the people of the north, the descendants of the sons of Israel, were such that it was not possible for monarchy or any institutions through which it might seek to relate itself to religious life to represent or adequately express loyalty to Yahweh. The same fundamental opposition to all monarchy that had caused the sons of Israel to reject Saul also had lain behind the revolution against David and the following of Sheba, and had enabled Jeroboam to break away from the Davidic kingdom after the death of Solomon—this same opposition violently erupted in reaction to the magnificent attempts of Omri and Ahab to do for the northern kingdom what David and Solomon had done for the south.

All this lies behind the opposition that centered on Jezebel in the reign of Ahab. For the devoted adherents of the older religion of Yahweh, as well as for those among them who were responsible for the accounts in which this opposition is described, the provisions made, in Samaria, for Jezebel's worship of the god Baal Melkart and for the functionaries of that god, epitomized what the policies of the house of Omri had led to.[16] It was not possible for Israel to condone such practices and, at the same time, to profess loyalty to Yahweh. Kingship as it was practiced by the house of Omri was incompatible with loyalty to Yahweh. A choice had to be made: either a return to the old purer ways of the fathers or the rejection of Yahweh for a kingship of the type being advanced by the house of Omri. There was no middle ground.

The uprising against the house of Omri, in which all this found expression, was stirred up and led by prophets—fanatical and unbending enthusiasts of the type that had given religious sanction to Jeroboam's split with the southern kingdom earlier. The movement which resulted in the fall of the house of Omri in 842 B.C. is, therefore, commonly referred to as the "prophetic revolution." With it are associated the names of two prophets in particular, Elijah and Elisha. Some of the most dramatic stories in the Old Testament are associated with them.[17] Out of this revolution came the impetus to commit to writing that strand of Old Testament thought that originated in the ancient confederation of the sons of Israel in which great stress was laid upon law and covenant and upon the role of Moses as the giver of the law by which Israel should order her life.[18]

For Israel law was not primarily a series of legal regulations. *Torah*—the Hebrew word—meant more than law in the narrower sense of the word. It was instruction in the direction life should take, based upon decisions taken in specific situations. It was given in those decisions through which the life of Israel assumed a character commensurate with its obligation to Yahweh.[19] In the kingdom of the south David had been able to bring about such a marriage of the religion of Yahweh and the monarchy that it was taken for granted that the king, and the priests and officials who were the extension of his person, could be the means through which Yahweh gave torah. There it was through the institution of kingship itself that the religion of Yahweh was related to the situation in which Yahweh's people were living when history made monarchy necessary. Passages such as II Samuel 7 and Psalms 2 and 110 witness to the way in which kingship was thoroughly integrated at Jerusalem with Israelite faith in Yahweh.

In the north, however, this was not possible. Because of opposition to Canaanite city-kingdoms and the demand of the covenant for exclusive loyalty to Yahweh, the old tribal confederation had been suspicious of kingship. And every encounter of the successors of the sons of Israel with what appeared to them to be royal pretension—their differences with David, their resentment of the grandeur of Solomon's reign, their refusal to do homage to Rehoboam—had only confirmed them in their conviction. With regard to monarchy they were thoroughgoing reactionaries. When, therefore, the house of Omri sought really to establish a monarchy, there was revolt. Torah, if it really originated with Yahweh, could never come through a king. It was not for a king to define the principles by which the life of Israel was to be ordered. For a king to do that was sheer presumption, a point of view which the stories told about Elijah epitomize.[20]

Such was the theological significance of the overthrow of the house of Omri and of the accession of a new dynasty in Jehu, a king chosen and approved by the prophetic party. The party responsible for the revolt was also responsible, in the years that followed, for some of the most important literature of the Old Testament. In this literature they emphasized their conviction that the law, the torah, by which the life of Israel was ordered, originated with no king. That law originated in the covenant graciously granted by Yahweh to Israel through Moses. What, therefore, the figure of David had come to be in the south as the symbol of the institution through which Yahweh continued to order the life of his people, Moses was to those in the north who opposed the pretensions of the house of Omri. It was in connection with the sentiment behind the prophetic revolution that the strands of the Old Testament in which Moses as lawgiver and covenant loyalty to Yahweh are emphasized came to be written down. This is not to say that the writings about to be mentioned were all written at the precise time of the revolution; they were more likely to have originated in the years between that revolution and the period after the fall of the northern kingdom to the Assyrians (850-700 B.C.). During these years the point of view of the party responsible for the revolution became increasingly reactionary and fanatical, and it regarded the fall of Samaria as divine confirmation of its attitude toward kingship.

THE ELIJAH AND ELISHA STORIES

When, under David's rule, the united kingdom had been successfully established, the first literature of that kingdom, we have seen, was most likely a narrative which celebrated the prowess and heroism of the king. But no king was the hero of the literature most immediately connected with the revolution in the north in the ninth century B.C. Rather, the literature most immediately connected with that revolution consists of two cycles of stories in which Elijah and Elisha are celebrated as the heroes who drove the pretentious Omriads from the throne (I Kings 17—II Kings 13).

The Elijah and Elisha stories make it quite clear that the romanticism and legend which had centered around David in the south came, in the north, to be connected with prophetic figures. Particularly is this true of the Elisha stories with their accounts of wonders and miracles. To see the difference between the spirit that motivated the followers of David in Jerusalem (in the tenth century B.C.) and the spirit that motivated the descendants of the sons of Israel in the north (in the ninth and eighth centuries), one has only to contrast the legends of the rise to power of the youthful David (e.g. I Samuel 16-18) with the legends about Elisha (II Kings 4 ff.). Romantic legends are always tributes to the greatness of their heroes, but they also always tell a good deal about the people who developed them. There was a great difference between the people whose hero had been a dashing, pure, fearless young warrior and those whose hero was a dour, pious, wonder-working old prophet.

If the stories about Elisha were the romantic manifestoes of the northern revolutionary party, the stories about Elijah served both as tributes to the single-minded devotee of Yahweh who started the revolt, and as dramatizations of the real issues at stake as the revolutionaries saw them. Elijah apparently appeared during the reign of Ahab, probably some few years before 850 B.C. and a decade before the successful completion of the revolution against the house of Omri. His dress and manner of life, as well as his message, were reminders to Israel that her origins and faith lay in a past vastly different from what she had become under the house of Omri. Elijah's call was an uncompromising one. Israel must choose between the loyalty to Yahweh demanded by the old covenant and what the house of Omri represented. There was no middle ground.

The Elijah stories are, then, evidence equally for the issues of the time as seen by the revolutionaries as for the course of events in the time of Elijah. They reflect both the message of that prophet and the position of his followers. The life of Israel, they are saying, cannot, if Israel is to be loyal to Yahweh, be ordered by the torah of a king. The life of Israel must be ordered by Yahweh to whom, under the covenant, Israel owes exclusive allegiance.

It is not without significance that the stories recount that in a crisis in his career Elijah betook himself to the mountain in the desert where the covenant had been given, there to receive encouragement and further inspiration. The fact that it was at that mountain that Elijah received the commission to see that Jehu was anointed king is symbolic of the ultimate origins of the prophetic revolution in the covenant theology of the sons of Israel. Israel may have come to a point where having a king was inevitable, but only the king anointed by a prophet such as Elisha, successor to the great Elijah, would be acceptable. The king in Israel must be inferior to the covenant loyalty demanded by Yahweh, to the law given by Moses, to the prophetic successors of Moses.

THE E DOCUMENT

Just as the J Document had, in the early days of the southern kingdom, gone behind the legends about the rise of the monarchy to seek its ultimate sources, so the sentiment behind the prophetic revolution in the north found expression in literature that probed further back than Elijah and Elisha. The J Document, it was pointed out earlier, was clearly the creation of a southerner,[21] concerned to relate and recount the traditions of the whole of Israel, but from the point of view of one who knew those traditions as they were preserved in the south. Furthermore, so far as we can tell, the view of monarchy taken by the J Document was that typical of the south where the religion of Yahweh and Davidic kingship had been firmly allied.

The northern attempt, made sometime after the prophetic revolution and under the influence of that revolution, to find the origins of Israel was dependent upon the same traditions that lay behind the J Document. Furthermore, it was dependent upon those traditions as the J Document had related them to one another and as they had been molded by the process of unification which had preceded its writing. Yet this attempt was made by those who were concerned to preserve the distinctive emphases of northern Yahwism, particularly in the light of the threat recently posed by the house of Omri.

This northern version of the early traditions of Israel is called the E Document. Though some scholars would see it simply as a supplemented form of the J Document, it is more likely to have originated as a separate narrative. However, since the J and E Documents came to be interwoven with one another and later also combined with the Priestly Code, it is never possible to speak with absolute assurance on such matters. That should be borne in mind in connection with what follows.[22]

The E Document, or the school of thought which found expression in the E Document, is responsible for a narrative which, like the J narrative, runs from the beginning of Israel's history up into the time of the kingdoms.[23] But an examination of those portions of the Old Testament coming from the E source reveals a point of view quite different from that of J. The basis of both J and E is found in the national traditions of Israel, but the method of presenting those traditions and the points of emphasis differ significantly.

First of all, the E Document—at least what remains of it—does not begin with a creation story and does not contain any of those myths and legends of man's prehistory which the J Document used in order to relate the history of Israel to all of history. The E Document begins straightway with Abraham and with the promise that was the beginning of the history of the covenant people of Yahweh. The exclusiveness of E mirrors the position to which those responsible for the prophetic revolution and their successors were driven in their struggle against forces subversive of Yahwism. They were unable to see, as J had, any relation between Israel's own

The Witness of the Law 59

calling as the people of Yahweh and the rest of the nations. They were not able to relate their own history to history as a whole—except in terms of a true faith battling for survival against pagan threats.

E, then, is motivated by a more specifically religious interest than J. J was—even though it is anachronistic to use this analogy—a historian working with his sources. He not only put down the sometimes lusty stories of the ancestors of his people as they came to him, but seems to have enjoyed the stories for their own sake. Not so with E: a comparison of Genesis 12:10-20 (J) with Genesis 20 (E) will show how E tempers the more primitive description of God's way with the foreign ruler who takes Sarah. E tends to "clean up" the stories of the patriarchs. E also tends to have a more exalted and less primitive conception of God, having God speak through angels or dreams rather than appear directly. This is not to say that the writer of J was theologically inferior to the writers of E. It is more likely due to J's faithful reproduction of the stories and to E's preoccupation with a theological position.

The most distinctive portion of the E Document is that which describes the exodus and the events connected with it. Like J, E tells about the call of Moses and of the events that led to the escape from Egypt. But in E the role of Moses as the influential figure in the development of Israel's faith, indeed as the creator of that faith, is heavily emphasized. E, as opposed to J, even says that until the time of Moses the real identity and nature of God were not known. It was only to Moses that Yahweh revealed his name (Exodus 3:13-15). Whatever may be the reasons for this significant difference between J and E, it is quite clear that E emphasized the formative and authoritative role of Moses in order to assert that Yahweh had not worked to establish a people through any more recent institution such as kingship. It was through Moses and the ancient events in which he played the chief human part that Yahweh had acted.

J and E also differed in their accounts of the escape from Egypt. Apparently the legends about the plagues that came upon the Egyptians varied, and E recounted them in the northern version. Yet, despite the northern emphasis on the role of Moses, E told how the elders of Israel had been associated with Moses in his work and of how "judges" had been chosen to have part with him in the leadership of the people (Exodus 18). It is, however, in connection with the sojourn at the holy mountain that E added the most material to J.

Aside from the so-called cultic decalogue in Exodus 34 (probably a supplement to J) and Exodus 25-31 and 34:29 ff. (both from the Priestly Code), the legal material in Exodus comes from E. The prelude to this legal material is the famous decalogue of Exodus 20:1-17. The bulk of the law in E is a section, Exodus 20:22—23:33, into which an already extant code was incorporated. This section is usually referred to as the "Book of the Covenant." Exodus 24 is E's account of how Israel subscribed to the covenant. There, again, the covenant concept is emphasized as are the role of Moses and the inescapable obligation of Israel to live by the law given through Moses.

Read in the light of what had happened during the period of the dynasty of Omri, these emphases and differences take on new meaning. For E the will of God for Israel had been revealed in ancient times through Moses: it was there, in the law given through Moses, that Israel was to find the principle by which she should order her existence. To seek to find that principle in law given and administered by a king would be betrayal of her vocation. What Omri had sought to accomplish was blasphemy and apostasy.

It is very difficult to disentangle J and E in Numbers. At the point in the narrative, however, at which the conquest of Palestine is recounted, the E Document lays great stress on the wonderful way in which Yahweh led his people to victory over their enemies through a chosen leader such as Joshua. And the climax of E's account of Israel's occupation of her land is Joshua 24 where the renewal of the covenant at Shechem is recounted.

It is clear that, in all this, E is drawing upon the traditions of the old tribal confederation of the sons of Israel that had preceded the united monarchy. It is clear, too, that in opposition to what had happened under the house of Omri, E's purpose is to assert vigorously that it is to the past Israel must look to find out what she really is. It was from Yahweh himself, and through his servant Moses, that the law came by which Israel had to live in order really to be Israel.

The reason, then, for the emphasis on law and covenant in E was twofold. It came, in the first place, from the history behind the tribes and clans which eventually composed the northern kingdom, and it went back to the traditions of the sons of Israel, the tribal confederation antedating the Philistine invasion and the rise of Saul. It also went back to a people who cherished "states' rights," whose vigorous individualism and uncompromising loyalty to Yahweh made them suspicious of any new way or institution.

But the emphases of the E Document also find their cause in the more proximate historical situation. History having reached the point where Israel could no longer be a loose confederation, the house of Omri had attempted to make of Israel a strong and stable monarchy. The Omriads sought to accomplish this in political and physical terms and to provide institutions that would give to the monarchy prestige and religious status. Against this the descendants of the sons of Israel had revolted under the leadership of a prophetic party. The justification for the reactionary spirit of the prophetic party, as well as for the bloody *coup* which brought Jehu to power as king, was found in the fervent desire to return from the pagan innovations of the Omriads to the ancient covenant under which Israel had pledged absolute loyalty to Yahweh alone. This is what lies behind E's setting down the old confederation traditions, and this explains the emphasis in E on the law associated with the covenant and on Moses as the only authoritative lawgiver in Israel.[24]

Whether or not the E Document carried its account up through the founding of the kingdom by Saul, it is difficult to say, but we do find stories in I and II Samuel which contradict the point of view of the earliest narrative of the rise of the monarchy as given by J and which reflect the attitude of the E Document.[25] These stories are concerned to make it clear that monarchy in Israel was, from the very beginning, a defection from Yahweh. Furthermore, they insisted that, when Israel *had* demanded a king, the king was subject to the choice and control of the priestly seer Samuel. Through the figure of Samuel, as through the figures of Elijah and Moses, the people of the north were making clear their position that the king, if Israel did have to have one, must always be content with a secondary position. The primary commitment of Israel was to Yahweh, and that commitment found expression in the covenant given through Moses and in the law which spelled out the covenant obligations.

DEUTERONOMY

It is also in the line of tradition running from the ancient northern confederation of tribes to the prophetic revolution against the house of Omri that the ultimate origins of the book of Deuteronomy, the third of the four basic documents of the Pentateuch, are to be found. It is true that Deuteronomy came later to play an important role in the south, in Jerusalem. It is also true that the account of the reformation of Josiah in II Kings 22-23 is meant to connect Deuteronomy with the southern kingdom. Nevertheless, scholars are coming increasingly to see that the point of view of Deuteronomy is basically the same as that of the other Old Testament strata connected with the north.[26] Deuteronomy, like the Elijah and Elisha legends, the E Document, and the anti-monarchy parts of I Samuel, finds its ultimate origins in the faith of the sons of Israel. And it is extremely likely, although not capable of proof, that it first came to be written—although not in its final complete form—during those years in which opposition to the house of Omri prompted the north to give expression to its basic position.

Deuteronomy epitomizes the spirit of the covenant-law tradition of the Old Testament at its best. Except for its conclusion (chapter 34)—really the conclusion to the whole Pentateuch and not to Deuteronomy alone—it is cast in the form of pronouncements of Moses to Israel. Though the love of God and the necessity of love toward God are emphasized—Jesus' first and great commandment comes from Deuteronomy—there is nothing sentimental about the relationship between God and his people. An uncompromising loyalty to Yahweh is demanded. Though a number of the provisions of the code of Deuteronomy are surprisingly humanitarian, no quarter or mercy is shown the pagan peoples whose presence and religion were threats to Israel's loyalty to Yahweh.

Deuteronomy leaves no doubt that the law by which the life of Israel is to be ordered is the law given by Yahweh through Moses, and the fearful consequences of disobedience to that law are spelled out (cf. Deuteronomy 28:15-68). It is quite explicitly stated that law for Israel is not to be defined by the king, but that the king is to be subject to the law given through Moses (Deuteronomy 17:14-20). It is through obedience to the law given through Moses that Israel's life will be attended by blessing and peace (Deuteronomy 28:1-14).[27]

A RELIGION OF THE BOOK

For the J Document, history itself, with Israel as a part of it, was the chief witness to the lordship of Yahweh. In the course

God and History in the Old Testament

of events leading to the Davidic kingdom Yahweh's character and purpose had been revealed. It was, therefore, by narrative alone J could testify to the conviction that Yahweh was indeed God. There is a real sense in which the J Document was addressed to whoever would hear what it had to say. So far as Israel was concerned, the place where she was standing made sense, but the vitality of God and the movement of history made it impossible to spell out what course she must take in some new time and place.

For the E Document and Deuteronomy, as well as for the literature associated with their point of view, Yahweh was—as for J—known through the history in which he had been at work. There is no question but that both J and E go back to the same amalgam of traditions. The emphasis in E and Deuteronomy, however, is different. In the north, where the use of covenant and law to express the implications of Israel's relation to Yahweh had originated, the closeness and strength of Canaanite religion had forced the sons of Israel to be more definite in their assertion of the uniqueness of Hebrew faith. And, as time went on, no new institutions were "baptized," as David had "baptized" the cult and tradition of Jerusalem, so that faith in Yahweh might be related to new political and cultural situations. Thus, the more ardent and faithful northern adherents of Yahweh found themselves in opposition not only to paganism but to any attempt in Israel to create new institutions to provide a structure for Israel's life in new situations. Thus, too, those who sought to create such institutions were forced into a seemingly pagan position.

This constant tension drove the northern devotees of Yahweh to put increasing emphasis upon the ancient covenant obligations of Israel, spelled out in such codes as the Book of the Covenant (Exodus 20:22—23:33) and the code that underlies the present book of Deuteronomy. It was this tension, too, that drove them to an increasing veneration of Moses, particularly as the authoritative figure—more impressive than any king—through whom the covenant and the law had been given.

This tension reached its height when Omri and his successors decided to cut the Gordian knot and make of the northern kingdom what it had to be in order to have stability and security and prosperity—even if this meant a break with the past. In the ensuing struggle, the tendency to emphasize Moses and the law reached its peak. As opposed to the king, Moses was the giver of law in Israel. As opposed to pretentious royal institutions, the covenant law—now very definitely defined in a written form (cf. Exodus 24:3-8, Deuteronomy 17:18-20)—was that by which the life of Israel was to be ordered.

Thus, like the narrative of the Old Testament, the law witnessed to the sovereignty of the God who had revealed himself to Israel. The law, like the narrative, is part of an historical religion. Its claim to authority is based on its definition of the obligations of Israel in the light of the ancient events in which God had made himself known. Furthermore, just as more recent events had prompted the writing of the narrative, so more recent events—the policy of Omri— prompted the writing of the law.

The writing of the narrative, however, traced only the significance of the point to which Israel had arrived, and left the question of the future open. But the writing of the law provided a definitive statement of Israel's obligations in any age. It was the beginning of a religion of the book in which subsequent historical events would have meaning only as a setting in which Israel either obeyed or disobeyed the unchanging law. The written law would, on the one hand, be the sturdy backbone of a faith that endured tragedy and persecution and ridicule. It would, on the other hand, be the basis of a reactionary religious obscurantism prone to discredit prophetic discernment of new acts of God in the ongoing course of history.

CHAPTER THREE

The Witness of the Prophets

In addition to narrative and law, prophetic literature is a prominent feature of the Old Testament. Not only are there three large prophetic books—Isaiah, Jeremiah and Ezekiel—and twelve smaller ones, but there is also the quasi-prophetic book of Daniel.[1] Furthermore, Jewish tradition refers to the books from Joshua through II Kings as the "former prophets." Like the narrative and legal portions of the Old Testament, the prophetic books are the products of a long history. A conviction of the working of God in the events of history lay behind the books in the first place, and a conviction of the continuing work of God in subsequent history led to their being written down in their present form.

Prophecy was not limited to those men whose names have been attached to books. Behind the canonical prophets (the ones for whom books have been named) lies a long history. Prophets were, apparently, something with which the Hebrews came into contact when they settled Palestine.[2] They were religious figures, much like the whirling dervishes of present-day Islam, subject to seizures taken to be the work of a god. In the prophetic state they would sing, dance, and jabber—go through abnormal physical contortions. What "prophesying" could be in early times is shown by the use of the verb in I Samuel 18:10. When it is said of Saul, in earlier

English translations, that "he prophesied in the midst of the house," the meaning is clearly that Saul became irrational, that he raved—and so the word is translated in the Revised Standard Version.[3]

There is no doubt that those who prophesied in this sense were regarded in ancient times with the same suspicion and contempt with which religious fanatics have ever been regarded. Yet they were also respected, for the seizures to which they were subject were believed to be the result of the presence of a god. The prophetic frenzy was an "outward and visible sign" that a god was at hand.

Just as the Hebrews utilized other originally foreign religious institutions in their worship and service of Yahweh, so, after the settlement of Palestine, some of them became prophets of Yahweh. When a more settled way of life had resulted in the loss of some of the fervor of earlier days, when there were no longer those who, like the ancient judges, were subject to possession by the spirit of Yahweh, prophets provided an expression of that unpredictable coming of God and ecstatic surrender characteristic of former times. Though their mode of expression might have been borrowed from Canaanite holy men, the activity of these early Israelite prophets was the sign that Yahweh could still be present with the power by which he had won the land for his people. The prophets were Yahweh enthusiasts in a time when enthusiasm for Yahweh might wane in the face of the prestige and popularity of some of the Canaanite deities.

BANDS OF PROPHETS

It was particularly at the time of the Philistine threat that the prophets came to the fore to stir up the various elements of the sons of Israel and the house of Judah to the unity that alone could enable the Hebrews to hold their territory. Being a newer institution, the prophets would not have had the stake in the older *status quo* that held the priests of the northern confederation back from real endorsement of Saul's kingship. The prophets were supporters of the monarchy, and Saul's close connection with them gave rise to a popular proverb (I Samuel 10:9-13).

When the monarchy had become established, the prophets became a part of the royal court. Though the legend of his rebuke of David's behavior in the Bathsheba affair may be reading into earlier times the standards of later prophets, Nathan was closely associated with David. Indeed, in the struggle over the succession to David's throne, Nathan was a supporter of Solomon, the representative of the newer kind of kingship associated with the taking of Jerusalem. It was through the prophesying of court prophets that, to the minds of the ancient Israelites, Yahweh manifested his presence in and approval of the monarchy.

If there were pro-Davidic prophets, there were also prophets associated with those elements of the united monarchy not entirely happy with subjection to the king at Jerusalem. The stories have it that Ahijah, a prophet, proclaimed it to be the will of Yahweh that Jeroboam should establish a separate northern kingdom (I Kings 11:29-40). And in the northern kingdom, just as in the south, prophets were associated with the court. Their function—through the ecstasy with which they were seized—was to assure the king that the spirit of God was present in what he was doing or planning. The presence of God would be manifest in their dancing and singing and wild behavior. The spirit of God might also indicate more specific approval of some royal policy or undertaking through an oracle spoken by the prophet in his ecstatic state.

The way in which the court prophets functioned is shown very clearly in the story of Micaiah in I Kings 22. There, in spite of their separation, the kings of Israel and Judah are allied against a common enemy, the Syrians. Before undertaking the siege of a certain city, the kings consult the prophets to be sure that Yahweh is with them and that success will attend their venture. The way in which the prophets, acting communally under a leader, prophesy success for the royal undertaking in act and word is described:

> Now the king of Israel and Jehoshaphat the king of Judah were sitting each on his throne, arrayed in their robes, at the threshing floor at the entrance of the gate of Samaria; and all the prophets were prophesying before them. And Zedekiah the son of Chenaanah made for himself horns of iron, and said, "Thus says Yahweh, 'With these you shall push the Syrians until they are destroyed!' " And all the prophets prophesied so, and said, "Go up to Ramoth-gilead and triumph; Yahweh will give it into the hand of the king." (I Kings 22:10-12)

The function of the prophets is, quite clearly, to provide divine assurance of success for the kings' attack. This illustrates their role at the court. The kings who maintained them —while, perhaps somewhat superstitiously, respectful of the prophetic gifts—did not do so simply out of objective interest in what the divine will might be. It was hoped that the prophets might indicate divine approval of the will of the king.

THE EMERGENCE OF INDIVIDUAL PROPHETS

In the prophetic phenomenon, however, the Israelite kings got more than they bargained for. Through this institution, which by the middle of the ninth century had become well established as a means through which God spoke to his people, God began to say things contrary to the will of the king and contrary to the best interests of Israel as Israel saw them. The chief purpose of the story in I Kings 22 is not to show us how the court prophets normally functioned, but to introduce one of them whose "Thus says Yahweh . . ." does not agree with what the majority of the prophets are saying and is inimical to the purpose of the king. Micaiah, reluctantly and to his own discomfort and disadvantage, must speak the truth about the present situation as that truth has been revealed to him by Yahweh. And, he is convinced, that truth is contrary to what the king wants to hear and contrary to what the court prophets have been saying. The siege will not be successful, and the king of Israel will be slain.

The story of Micaiah involves simply a situation in which one prophet is convinced that the court prophets are wrong. Yet in it is seen the nature of prophecy as it existed even in the greatest of Israel's prophets. Prophecy is an institution through which, Israel believed, God could speak the truth about some specific situation or undertaking. Micaiah, in his outward appearance and manner, is undoubtedly a prophet in the sense in which "prophet" was understood in his time. To his hearers, therefore, what he says must be of God. Yet, what he says is not automatically to the advantage of Israel. He is speaking the truth about some historical situation because he has been inspired to do so by the God who is Lord of history. Thus, in Micaiah, the prophetic phenomenon is not primarily predictive, nor primarily a means of religious support for the king, but is becoming a vehicle through which the truth about some historical situation is verbalized. It is becoming the means whereby the word in which God defines the meaning of history is spoken. It is as such that prophecy in Israel is to be understood.

ELIJAH AND ELISHA

The previous chapter has indicated the decisive role played by the prophets of Yahweh in the revolution that removed the dynasty of Omri from the throne of the northern kingdom. Both the old and the new in prophetism are apparent in the stories about Elijah and Elisha. There is no doubt but that the phenomena associated with the ecstasy characteristic of the older kind of prophet was present in them. Elijah is able to perform feats requiring superhuman strength. His words to the prophets of Baal on Mount Carmel have the flavor of the kind of mocking, vengeful pronouncement typical of an earlier stage of prophecy. Both Elijah and Elisha are believed to be susceptible to seizure by the spirit of God, and, when so seized, are capable of wonderful and miraculous acts. Both can see things not visible to the eyes of ordinary men. And, Elisha in particular is associated with a band of prophets, with a professional group designated as "the sons of the prophets."

Yet the new element in prophetism manifest in the story of Micaiah is also manifest in the stories of Elijah and Elisha. Elijah is a solitary figure who comes forth to stand alone for Yahweh against the king. He is by no means simply the agency through which the monarchy is assured of divine support. Against everyone he is called to define the issue present in the attempt of Omri and Ahab to make of Israel a kingdom like those about her. And although Elisha and the band of prophets with which he is associated have much in common with the earlier prophets, they are, nonetheless, the successors of Elijah—not of court prophets. Theirs is not the task simply of bringing divine reassurance to the *status quo*. They are the means by which Yahweh overthrows one dynasty and brings another to power. When the revolution is finished and Jehu is king, the prophets are not, at least from the point of view of their party, the courtiers of the king. The king is the creation of the prophets.

The northern kingdom after the prophetic revolution was the most self-consciously pro-Yahweh institution that Israel had ever had. The enthusiastic loyalty of the old tribal confederation was present, but present with a vengeance. That loyalty was now a reactionary loyalty, called forth by opposition. And the return of the prophetic party to the ways of the premonarchical confederation was a self-conscious return that had about it the artificiality and defensiveness always present in some attempt to recover an idealized past.

The prophetic spirit that had brought the new dynasty of Jehu to power was, by its very insistence upon exclusive loyalty to Yahweh, a source of self-righteous satisfaction on the part of those who had turned out the house of Omri.[4] The demand that it had voiced was crystallized into a law. Thus, the place of Elijah and Elisha in the history of Israel's religion is more closely related to the developments discussed in the previous chapter than to the prophetic movement as such. They did not so much proclaim the meaning of some moment of history, as lead a reform. Their association with the rise of the dynasty of Jehu could make the ruling classes under that dynasty think of themselves as champions of the ways of God, and the prosperity in the north in the century following the revolution could be interpreted as a sign of divine approval of all that had been done. Both the prophetic leadership of the revolution and the return to the divine law were sources of self-righteous pride against which the first of the great canonical prophets, Amos, felt constrained to speak.[5]

THE HISTORICAL BACKGROUND OF THE PRE-EXILIC CANONICAL PROPHETS

To view Amos and his successors merely as reprovers of Israel, even in the least moralistic and most profoundly religious way, is to miss the primary point about the great canonical prophets. Like Micaiah, the great prophets were called to give voice to the truth present in history. It was their function to define the meaning of the history in which Israel was involved in a given present. Their ability to do this sprang from a knowledge of the God who reigned in history, a knowledge dependent upon what he had revealed of himself and his ways in past history. They knew what the issue of the historical situation must be because they knew him whose purpose gave history its meaning. That they knew God does not, however, mean that they were primarily concerned with moral or religious teaching or exhortation in any specialized sense. Because of the way in which the sacred and the secular are separated in our culture and thinking, it is very difficult for us to understand this. Indeed, anything we may say about it will be somewhat distorted. Nevertheless, there is a real sense in which the great prophets were more like news analysts than preachers. For them God was not a religious figure, but the Lord of history.

When, therefore, Amos, the first in a great succession, appeared, he was not simply a reprover of Israel, sent by God to tell his people what they ought to do or be.[6] He was a man to whom God had opened his counsel so that the divine purpose in history might be known to men. This he believed, as did those responsible for preserving what he said. He was, like his successors, one to whom God had vouchsafed that word in which the meaning of history is verbalized. His mission was to give voice to an "is" rather than an "ought." Someone, later than Amos, saw this, and summed it all up in a comment preserved in the book bearing Amos' name: "Surely the Lord God does nothing, without revealing his secret to his servants the prophets" (Amos 3:7).

Since it was in the historical events transpiring in their times —not in some static religious position—that the prophets discerned God at work giving the lie to the self-righteousness of his people and bringing his purpose to fulfillment, something of the historical background must be understood if the prophets are truly to be understood. And the historical background of the canonical prophets is nothing other than the period in which history was moving toward the annihilation of Israel as a national power. The message of the prophets becomes truly remarkable when it is seen that they discerned the sovereignty of God in the very events by which his people were being destroyed as a nation.

Only the fact that for a period of some five or six hundred years a political vacuum had existed in the ancient Near East made it possible for Israel, and other smaller nations, to become independent powers. From about 1200 B.C. until 600 B.C. neither Egypt nor any power at the Babylonian end of the Fertile Crescent was strong enough to dominate the arable land stretching around the northern edge of the Arabian Desert from the Nile to the Persian Gulf. It was in this period that the Philistines could establish themselves on the shores of the Mediterranean, that the Syrians (or Arameans) could establish a kingdom at Damascus, that the Edomites and the Moabites and the Ammonites could become independent. And it was in this period that Saul could summon the sons of Israel and the house of Judah to a unity on which David could build an empire.[7]

We have seen how the Old Testament began to come into being because Israel did not interpret the situation which had made it possible for her to be an independent nation in sheerly political terms. It was, for the framers of the Old Testament narrative, no accident that a vacuum existed in the ancient Near East in which Israel could become a national power. The whole thing was the result of providence. Those responsible for the stories in which the rise of David is celebrated in a romantic and adulatory way might say this in a shallowly nationalistic way. The J Document might interpret the situation more profoundly as the work of God in order to make it possible for the people who had come to know him in the exodus and the events associated with it to witness to their knowledge before the world. Nevertheless, both were maintaining that the course of events in the world of which Israel was a part had meaning in terms of the God who reigned in and through those events. The existence of Israel as a nation was the evidence of this.

Beginning about 750 B.C., however, the power vacuum that had existed in the ancient Near East since about 1200 began to be filled up. The Assyrians, a people whose home was found on the upper Tigris River and who had been a power for a long time, began at that time to move westward in a decisive way. Indeed, it was only the preoccupation of the Assyrians with the Syrians, Israel's neighbors to the north, that accounted for the period of peace and prosperity preceding the appearance of Amos and Hosea and gave self-righteous Israelites reason to believe that God was rewarding their faithfulness to him.

It was the expansion of Assyria to the west, an expansion that was the dominant fact in Near Eastern history for over a century, that was the background against which Amos, Hosea, Isaiah, Micah, and Zephaniah lived and prophesied. It was that expansion that completely destroyed the northern kingdom in 721 B.C. and which reduced the southern kingdom to a vassal state consisting only of Jerusalem and her immediately outlying territory.

By about 620 B.C., Assyria had established control over all the territory from Mesopotamia to the Mediterranean and had even marched into Egypt, but thereafter she went into a rapid decline. In 612 B.C. Nineveh, her capital city, fell to the combined forces of the Medes and the Babylonians. The fall of Assyria did not, however, bring an end to attempts to fill the ancient Near Eastern power vacuum. Babylonia, first under Nabopolassar and then under the biblically famous Nebuchadrezzar, defeated an attempt of Egypt to succeed to the Assyrian power, and established herself as the successor to Assyria.

What had begun, for the Israelites, with the Assyrians was finished by the Babylonians. A siege of Jerusalem in 598-97 B.C. led to the surrender of the Davidic king and to the deportation of the royal house and the ruling families to Babylonia. A revolt by those Israelites left in Palestine led to another Babylonian invasion and to the fall of Jerusalem in 587. All that Saul and David had started was now gone. There was no longer an Israelite state. The territory of the former northern kingdom had been depopulated earlier by the Assyrians. The leaders of the southern kingdom were in exile. A leaderless and poverty stricken population was left in Palestine. The land lay waste and the temple and most of Jerusalem were in ruins. It was through the period of uncertainty and upheaval and invasion and destruction that attended the fall of Assyria and the rise of Babylonia that Nahum, Jeremiah, and Ezekiel lived and prophesied. Tradition also places Habakkuk in this period.[8]

THE MESSAGE OF THE
PRE-EXILIC PROPHETS

So it was that the century and a half during which the great, pre-exilic prophets appeared was a period of cataclysmic historical change for the ancient Near East. Moreover, it was, for Israel, the end of national existence. The wave of history on whose crest Israel had become a great kingdom had rolled on, and its breaking had dashed Israel to bits. It was precisely in the midst of that end and of the breaking of that wave that the canonical prophets were present and active.

There is no doubt but that these great prophets functioned in much the same way as their predecessors had. This is to say that the "format" of their prophesying was not radically different from that of the band of prophets present in the Micaiah story. They were subject to ecstatic seizures. They beheld strange visions. They spoke in frenzied and rhythmic oracles. They might perform peculiar symbolic actions. Though, like Amos, the great prophets might vigorously deny that they were "professionals"—might disclaim any connection with the earlier type of prophet—they could only describe their call as a call to "prophesy" (cf. Amos 7:14-15). Indeed, given the content of their message, the only thing that gained any hearing at all for them was the fact that their outward appearance and *modus operandi* were those of "prophets." Given the time and culture, it was the presence of "prophetic inspiration" in the earlier and more primitive sense that convinced the great prophets themselves, as well as those around them, that God had had something to do with what they were saying.[9]

What distinguished the great canonical prophets from their predecessors was not their mode of expression, but what they had to say. And there is no doubt that the content of the prophets' message was dependent upon the faith to which the J Document had given expression.[10] J had looked back over the long and complex history leading to the establishment of the Davidic monarchy, and had found that the thing that held the various elements in that history together and that explained that history's meaning was the sovereignty in and through it of Yahweh, the God who had revealed himself to Israel. The prophets looked out upon the historical present in which the rise and expansion of great empires was bringing to pass a new and different Near East as well as finishing the existence of the remnants of the Davidic empire. As the sovereignty of Yahweh had explained past history to J, so that sovereignty explained present history for the prophets. In the tradition of the J Document, the great prophets were not constructing a religion or a theology. They were witnessing to the lordship over the events of their own time of the God who had revealed himself to Israel in past events. For them the rise of the great empires did not mean that Yahweh had abdicated or that he was powerless before the Assyrian or Babylonian gods. Precisely through the destroyers of the nation he had brought into being was Yahweh manifesting his rule: Ah, Assyrian, the rod of my anger! (Isaiah 10:5)

A unique kind of God had appeared in the prophets' pronouncements. This Yahweh was no religious figure, rising and then falling with the fortunes of his devotees. Either the prophets were hopelessly deluded or they had been admitted to a knowledge of the one who really is God.

Thus a primary assertion of the pre-exilic prophets was that the course of history had to be accepted. The story of Israel from the time of the rise of the Assyrians to the time of the fall of Jerusalem is, politically, the story of countless attempts to stay, through one means or another, the fate that obviously lay in store for the two little Palestinian kingdoms.[11] For the prophets these attempts were vain not only because of the inexorable sweep of historical events but because of the way in which those events were—however terribly and mysteriously —moving toward the accomplishment of the purpose of the very God who had chosen Israel. Any attempt of Israel to escape the situation in which she found herself or to change the course of history was an attempt to escape from her God and to thwart his reign in history. (Cf. Isaiah 30:1-5)

For the canonical prophets, therefore, the only area in which Israel could know and confess her God was the historical present. It was of this present that he was Lord. It was to it that history had been moving. It was in it that he was now acting. For the prophets it was not what Israel *had* been in the days of Moses or David that counted—although in what she had been through was to be found the clue to what she must be now. For the prophets Israel's status as the people chosen to witness to the sovereignty of God had to be defined in terms of the present. Yahweh's sovereignty was a living thing, not something that could be captured simply in the remembrance of things past—even though it was the remembrance of the past in which the fact of his sovereignty was made clear.

It is out of such conviction, conviction entirely in line with the point of view of the J Document, that the prophetic condemnations of Israel arise. Those condemnations are, in terms of their basic purpose, neither moralistic nor hortatory. They are not the pronouncements of reformers whose primary task is to persuade Israel to mend her ways. They are definitions of what the present, and Israel in it, really are. And in these condemnations the prophets came into conflict with two things.

First of all—and this was particularly true in the north—the prophets came into conflict with the self-satisfaction of a people who honored Moses and the law and who believed that the people who did so could not be harmed. The reactionary piety, in which law and covenant figured so prominently, of a people who had, under prophetic leadership, overthrown the pagan pretensions of an Omri is the background of Amos' denunciations of the northern kingdom. The very concepts and traditions in which the demand of Yahweh for exclusive loyalty had found expression had become the basis of a smug complacency. The day is coming, Amos asserts, in which history will bring to Israel, in judgment, *God's* definition of justice and righteousness. *That* is the meaning of the present.

Secondly—and this was particularly true of the south where the house of David continued to reign—the prophets came into conflict with the ambitions of a people who saw themselves primarily not as those chosen to witness to the righteous sovereignty of Yahweh, but as a world power whose status as such had to be maintained whatever the cost to integrity might be. For the prophets—as for the writer of the J Document— the essential meaning of the existence of Israel was that the God who had revealed his sovereignty and power and righteousness in the exodus had called her to be the people who witnessed to him. That was why she had found herself in possession of a homeland. That was why the disparate elements of which she was composed had become a united people. That was why she had become a kingdom.

Israel, however, had forgotten all this. Israel, in the increasingly turbulent years from 750 to 600 B.C., was ordering her life as if the meaning of her existence lay solely in her being a nation. This, from the prophetic point of view, was the basic tragedy of which unrighteousness and corruption and apostasy were only manifestations.

> Israel is swallowed up;
>> Now they've become
> As a vessel among the nations
>> That's of no use at all. (Hosea 8:8)

Israel's attempt, the prophets were saying, to define the meaning of history and her place in it had vitiated her usefulness for the purpose for which Yahweh had brought her into being.

For the prophets, therefore, the meaning of the expansion of Assyria and, later, of Babylonia—the most notable developments between 750 and 600 B.C.—lay in the fact that Yahweh was at work as he had been continually in the history of Israel. If, by faithfulness to the purpose for which he had called her into being, given her a homeland, and made of her a kingdom, Israel would not witness to Yahweh's righteous sovereignty, then, however much she might vainly struggle to have it otherwise, she would witness to his righteous sovereignty by being judged. If his people would not witness to him by ordering their life in accord with his righteousness, then his righteousness would have to be manifest in the terrible destiny history was about to mete out to them in terms of the westward expansion of the Mesopotamian empires. One way or another, history would demonstrate that the God who had made himself known to Israel was God, indeed. Neither the experience of having been chosen by him nor the possession of the institutions through which his past actions were remembered could save a people from the consequences of that fact. Israel was doomed.

THE PRESERVATION AND CONTINUATION
OF PROPHECY

The canonical prophets were not the authors of books. Even though what they were and did and said transformed the meaning and significance of prophetic inspiration, the way in which they functioned was not different in kind from that of their thoroughly ecstatic predecessors. The insight into the the meaning of history vouchsafed to them was conveyed to their contemporaries in terse, allusive, usually poetic oracles. Sometimes they were so overcome by the impending doom they saw for Israel that their conviction was conveyed in peculiar symbolic actions. But they were not the authors of books, even though an Isaiah or a Jeremiah might have some record made of what he had said.[12]

Nor were the prophets very much honored or heeded in their own times. Tradition has it that Isaiah was martyred by being sawn asunder, and the story preserved in Amos 7 seems to indicate that he was unceremoniously ejected from the sanctuary at Bethel. It was only when the course of history had shown that the prophetic interpretation of events, and not the interpretations of either reactionary Israelite piety or deluded Israelite nationalism, was right that the impetus to preserve the sayings of the prophets came.

It is difficult to imagine the enormity of the shock that the fall of Jerusalem was to the ancient Israelites. The event was not merely one in which their country had fallen to a foreign conqueror and their capital city, considered impregnable, had been laid waste. The independence of Israel in the land given her by her God and the continuing worship of that God in the temple at Jerusalem were foundation stones of Israelite faith. When, in 587 B.C., the Babylonian armies marched homeward, everything that Israel had been was gone. The heir of David was in exile in Babylonia. With him the leaders of the community languished, separated from the promised land and from the temple. In Palestine a leaderless and dispirited and decimated population faced an unknown and bleak future. The bottom had fallen out of Israel's existence. History had given the lie to everything she held dear. Was there any meaning in it all?

Only in terms of what the prophets had said did the situation in which Israel found herself have any meaning. If what the prophets had seen as the meaning of the rise and expansion of Assyria and Babylonia was true, if the dire tragedy that had overtaken the nation was a judgment of God, then it was not uncaring, purposeless fate that had struck Israel down. If

what the prophets had been saying about the state to which
Israel had been reduced was true, then the tragedy by which
Israel had been overtaken—while no less tragic—was re-
deemed from sheer meaninglessness. What had happened, terrible though it was, had happened because Israel's God was
still sovereign in history. It had happened because of the in-
exorably righteous purpose which gave all history its meaning.

In such terms did the prophets become comforters to Israel,
in some cases long after their words had been spoken and
long after they themselves had died or been martyred without
honor. What they did to lend meaning to the fall of Israel was
what provided the impetus to preserve their words. They were
worthy of remembrance because in retrospect they were seen
to have been discerners of the signs of the times.

So, in circles in which the prophetic spirit continued to live,
the prophets were honored and their words remembered. So,
in such circles, the message of the prophets was transmitted to
succeeding generations. The aim of such circles was to hand
down not merely the form of the prophet's words, but the living witness to God's lordship over history which the great
prophet had borne. Where it was necessary to interpret or to re-
apply the prophetic word so that its implications might be clear
to later hearers, the circles in which the prophets were remembered did so. The lesson that God had impressed upon the
prophets in their times was the lesson which, in any time, provided the clue to the meaning of history.

The books of the prophets, as they are now found in the
Old Testament, are the literary deposits of the orally transmitted tradition of such circles. It is when we read them as
such, understanding that they were never meant to be logically
or chronologically organized treatises, that we appreciate them
for what they are. It is when we read them as such, appreci-
ating not only the contribution of the original prophet but also
the contributions of his interpreters, that we begin to under-

stand the way in which the Old Testament has come into being over a period of centuries as a witness to the faith of those who, in divers times and places, have found that history makes sense in terms of the God who revealed himself to Israel and that the one true God makes himself known in terms of the purpose in which all history finds its meaning. Each of the prophetic books is, really, an anthology of faith having its origin in the prophet for whom it is named.

The prophetic circles, both in exile and in Palestine, were not, however, merely preservers and interpreters of the message of the great pre-exilic prophets. In them prophecy continued to live. From them came consolation and encouragement for defeated and discouraged Israel. It was, from the prophetic point of view, the purpose of God that had resulted in Israel's defeat and dispersion. It was the purpose of God that gave history its meaning. If, therefore, the meaning of history was to be found in the purpose of the sovereign God and not in the success or fortunes of Israel, then the end of Israel as a nation was not the end of purpose in history. In the purpose of God there was a future:

> Thus says the Lord God: It is not for your sake, O house of Israel, that I am about to act, but for the sake of my holy name . . . (Ezekiel 36:22)

So it was not on the basis of wishful thinking or merely sentimental daydreams, but on the basis of a solid faith in the sovereignty of the Lord God over history, that the successors of the great pre-exilic prophets called Israel away from yearning for a past that was gone or from purposeless accommodation to a confusing present to hope for the future. In the history now past the Lord God had revealed his righteousness and the power with which his righteousness was undergirded, had made clear to the eyes of faith the certainty of his sovereignty. But history was not complete. With the consistency that would make his work recognizable to those who knew of his former acts but with the wonderful newness that came of his being the living God, Israel's Lord was still at work. Thus, the prophetic books consist not only of remembrance of the great prophets and of interpretation and application, but also of later living prophecy.

THE RISE OF PERSIA AND THE CLIMAX OF THE PROPHETIC MOVEMENT

The hegemony of Babylonia in which Israel found herself a separated and exiled and subject people was not the concluding chapter in the turbulent history of the ancient Near East. Slightly more than half a century after she had defeated Assyria and slightly less than half a century after she had destroyed Jerusalem, Babylonia found herself facing a threat that was to be her downfall. To the east of Mesopotamia, in Persia, Cyrus had come to power. In the decade following 550 B.C. this Elamite ruler consolidated his position at home and skirted the Fertile Crescent to the north, enclosing the entire Semitic world in a pincers that reached from the Indian Ocean to the Halys River. By 540 B.C. he had turned toward Babylonia, and that city and the empire controlled by her rulers fell into his hands.[13]

In two ways the coming of Cyrus was a revolutionary thing, not only for the Babylonian empire, but for its subject peoples. First, Cyrus' coming introduced an entirely new factor into the area in which either Egypt or a Mesopotamian power had been dominant for centuries. The security lent by well-defined horizons, even when there are ups and downs inside those horizons, was shaken. The entrance of Persia into the picture brought strange and new peoples and tongues and ways into the ken of the Semitic peoples.

Second, Cyrus purposely reversed the policy of deportation of conquered peoples from their homelands, a policy by which the Babylonians and their Assyrian predecessors had sought to do away with possible centers of revolt. Cyrus allowed exiled peoples to return to their native lands, and even became a restorer and patron of native cults whose temples had been desecrated and looted by the Babylonians. He was an astute conqueror who cast himself in the role of a deliverer of his subjects and so made his conquest the more efficient and thorough.[14]

From the point of view of national or personal perspective and interest, then, the coming of the Persians under Cyrus brought uncertainty as well as the possibility of restoration and gain. In a new time history was moving along in the way that it ever does, denying the finality claimed by any *status quo*. Wherein was the meaning of this new turn of events to be found?

It was in answer to this question that there came a new upsurge of the prophetic spirit in the circle which owed its origin to the career of Isaiah of Jerusalem some two centuries before. It was in this upsurge that the climax of the prophetic movement came and that the prophetic point of view received its most explicit expression. That portion of the book of Isaiah in which there have been collected the magnificent poetic pronouncements of the prophets who responded to the action of God in the rise of Persia is referred to as Second or Deutero Isaiah, and it consists of chapters 40 through 55. Isaiah 40-55 is a much more polished literary production than any of the other prophetic writings, and in its finished form is probably the result of the work of some genius in the prophetic circle years after the time of Cyrus. The final portion of the book of Isaiah, chapters 56-66, reflects a still later stage in the life of the circle that originated with Isaiah, and it is commonly referred to as Third or Trito Isaiah.[15]

From the prophetic point of view the meaning of the rise of Cyrus and the coming of the Persians was not to be found in the overturn of accustomed ways and conditions. Neither was it to be found in the advantage that the seemingly magnanimous, but actually very shrewd, policies of Cyrus might bring to given individuals or national groups. From the prophetic point of view, the meaning of the rise of Cyrus and the coming of Persia lay, as did the meaning of history at its every point and in its totality, in the purpose of the God who was sovereign in history. Whatever might be the point of view of the Babylonian rulers or of the subject Jews or of Cyrus himself, this was the truth about what was transpiring.

Just as the escape of a band of Hebrew nomads from detention at the hands of mighty Egypt had been no lucky accident, just as the finding of a homeland by those nomads had been no mere stroke of good fortune, just as the unification of the Hebrews and the emergence of the Davidic empire had had more than just political and economic significance, just as the collapse of Israel as a national power had been the result of more than meaningless fate—so now the rise of Cyrus and the expansion of Persia had a meaning that mere national, or personal, self-interest could not exhaust:

> Who stirred up one from the east
> whom victory meets at every step? . . .
> Who has performed and done this,
> calling the generations from the beginning?
> I, Yahweh, the first,
> and with the last; I am he. (Isaiah 41:2,4)

It is quite clear that the prophetic proclamation in Isaiah 40-55 does not see the events of the years following 540 B.C. in isolation. Those events are recognized for what they really are on the basis of a point of view about history learned from the J Document and from former generations of the prophetic movement.[16] God is recognized in the historical present because of the way in which he has revealed himself in the past. It is the clue provided by Israel's past history that unlocks the meaning of the present through which she is passing. Thus the "new thing" happening with the coming of Cyrus is recognized for what it is in the purpose of God because of the "former things." Nowhere is the solidly historical nature of biblical faith more evident than in Second Isaiah.

Yet, in typical prophetic fashion, the "former things," the past, are not important in their own right. Their importance lies in the whole of which they are a part. The meaning of any part of history lies not in itself but in that fulfillment of the purpose of God toward which history is moving:

> Remember not the former things,
> nor consider the things of old.
> Behold, I am doing a new thing;
> now it springs forth, do you not perceive it?
> (Isaiah 43:18-19)

What then is the "new thing"? It is not the punishment of Babylonia for which defeated Israel might have yearned. It is not the might of Cyrus before which Israel and her contemporaries might be fearful and awe-stricken. It is not the advantage that the policy of Cyrus will bring to Israel. It is a return of exiled and homeless and hopeless and undeserving Israel to her homeland. Just as what had happened of old at the sea of Egypt had found its real meaning as a revelation of who it was who was God and of his righteous and saving purpose, so what was happening now found its real meaning in the return of Israel—in a new exodus—through which Yahweh would once again reveal his sovereignty and the goodness of his purpose for men:

> Go forth from Babylon, flee from Chaldea,
> declare this with a shout of joy, proclaim it,
> Send it forth to the end of the earth;
> say, "Yahweh has redeemed his servant Jacob!"
> (Isaiah 48:20)

It is in the glad shout of a rescued people that the meaning of history in 538 B.C. is revealed from the prophetic point of view.

It is in Second Isaiah that the implications of what the J Document and the prophets had said about the sovereignty of the God who had revealed himself to Israel are most explicitly stated. The exile and the way in which involvement in Babylonian culture and the coming of Persia had brought the prophets into contact with other religions caused the question of the relation of Israel's God to other gods to be raised. In Second Isaiah the conviction that only Israel's God is worthy of the name is reached and expressed in terms of sarcastic ridicule of other deities.[17] The other so-called gods are empty shams. The only reality they have is that of the stone and wood and metal of which their symbols are formed.

The prophetic conviction that only Israel's God is God is not, however, reached by a process of logical reasoning the end of which is a theoretical monotheism. Nor is it arrived at on the basis of sheerly religious considerations. It is not because Israel's God is more religiously satisfying that he is God alone. For the prophets the reason that Yahweh alone is entitled to be confessed as God is that he alone has given an adequate revelation of the meaning of history. Before the upheaval brought about by the coming of Cyrus the other so-called gods are mute, confounded. It is because the purpose he has revealed to his people alone makes sense of history that Israel's God is God indeed.

> I stirred up one from the north, and he has come,
>> from the rising of the sun, and he shall call on my name;
> he shall trample on rulers as on mortar,
>> as the potter treads clay.
> Who declared it from the beginning, that we might know,
>> and beforetime, that we might say, "He is right"?
> There was none who declared it, none who proclaimed,
>> none who heard your words.
> I have first declared it to Zion,
>> and I give to Jerusalem a herald of good tidings.
> But when I look there is no one;
>> among these there is no counselor
>> who, when I ask, gives an answer.
> Behold, they are all a delusion;
>> their works are nothing;
>> their molten images are empty wind. (Isaiah 41:25-29)

And because he is Lord of history, he is God of all things:

> Yahweh is the everlasting God,
>   the Creator of the ends of the earth. (Isaiah 40:28)

Thus the prophets, the climax of whose message is found in Second Isaiah, make it quite clear that the interest of the Old Testament is no narrowly religious interest. What the prophets had to say, like the message of the J Document, is not directed just to those whose interest runs to religious things or to Israel or to the Church. It is directed to the world. It involves the meaning of the world and its history. Its claim is to a knowledge of the one who is Lord of all things.

The culmination of the prophetic upsurge that produced Second Isaiah came, therefore, in the vision of a servant who would bring justice—the word has to do with living rightly ordered—to the nations and whose submission to suffering would be the perfect acknowledgment of God's sovereignty and would bring all men to a recognition of the truth.[18] That servant is, at one and the same time, all that Israel had been called to be from the beginning, and all that the prophets had been called to be.

CHAPTER FOUR

The Witness
of the Priestly Synthesis

The prophetic application of the faith, enunciated first in the J Document, to the events that had brought about the downfall of Israel made it possible for Israel to look forward to some kind of future. The God who had made himself known to Israel, so asserted the J Document and the prophets, was no merely religious deity of the type that rises and falls with the fortunes of his devotees. The God who had revealed himself was the only God, because his purpose alone explained the course of history. His purpose had not, therefore, either run out its course or been defeated in the collapse of Israel as a nation. Indeed, it was in his purpose that the collapse found meaning. The question, then, was not one of finding something new to replace that purpose of God which, up to this point, had been the justification of Israel's existence. The question presented by the downfall of Israel and by the prophetic interpretation of it had to do with the way in which Israel must find its place in that purpose under new and changed conditions.

Neither the J Document, in which the historical faith of Israel found its first and formative expression, nor the prophets had formulated programs for Israel. For them, by implication at least, the program with which Israel ought to be concerned was the program of God unfolding in the ongoing course of history. For them what God had vouchsafed to Israel was not a program that Israel was to follow, but a revelation of, and a relationship with, himself, in which his program would make sense as it did unfold. The question, therefore, of the place Israel was to find in the new situation brought about by her downfall as a nation was one which the prophets had raised but to which they had given no detailed answer. Even in Second Isaiah, where the rise of Persia is seen as the work of God to enable exiled Israel to return to her homeland, no detailed answer is given. It was from other than prophetic circles that programmatic answers to the question were to be developed.

THE PALESTINIAN COMMUNITY

At the fall of Jerusalem in 587 B.C. all Israel was not exiled to Babylon. The Babylonians were concerned, chiefly, to remove from Palestine any potential leadership of opposition or revolt. Accordingly, the exilic community consisted of the royal household and officials associated with it: military and other leaders, scribes and officials, and—significantly for the development of the Old Testament—the priests of the royal sanctuary, the Jerusalem temple. Since those who considered the exilic community the most significant portion of Israel during the period preceding the reconstruction of the temple in the years after 520 B.C. are responsible for the final form of the Old Testament, it is easy to assume that the exilic community was all there was of Israel.

A considerable number of Israelites, however, had been left in Palestine after the completion of the Babylonian invasion.[1] Indeed, it is extremely likely that, to the north of Jerusalem, survivors of the Assyrian destruction of the northern kingdom in 721 B.C. were still to be found. Those left in the southern part of Palestine after 587 B.C., and certainly any survivors of the northern kingdom, would not have associated Israel's faith as closely with the monarchy and the Jerusalem temple as did the exiled Israelites. Their answer to the question of what course Israel was now to take would be considerably different from that of those more closely connected with the house of David and the cult of the temple.

It was, therefore, to the interpretation of Israel which had originated in the old, premonarchical confederation of the sons of Israel and which had been championed and more definitely enunciated in the prophetic revolution against the house of Omri that these Palestinian Israelites seem to have turned. It is easy to understand how the emphases of that interpretation of Israel's faith would have seemed reasonable in the light of what had happened. That interpretation had always held that the life of Israel in her covenant relationship with her God must be ordered by the law given through Moses, not through monarchy or any post-Mosaic deviation from the purer original faith of Israel. It had only accepted monarchy with grave reservations, and had, in its version of the rise of the kingdom, interpreted Israel's wish to have a king as rebellion against her God.[2]

So now, when the kingdom of Saul and David had been divided for three and a half centuries, when the northern offshoot of that kingdom had gone down before the Assyrians a century and a third before, and when the southern kingdom had fallen to the Babylonians, it might well have appeared that the E Document and the Deuteronomic code and the tradition that they represented were right after all. Israel had had no business being a kingdom in the first place. David might have been a great man, but with few exceptions his successors —both in the south and in the north—had violated the law by which Moses had called Israel to live. The fall of the north and the subsequent fall of Jerusalem were only the judgment of God upon a people who had failed to keep his law. Israel must now return, chastened and humbled and stripped of her monarchical pretensions, to the kind of life that had preceded the kingdom.

There was thus a definitely antiquarian side to the program for Israel envisaged in the Palestinian part of the community. There was a concern to learn as much as possible about what Israel had been like and of the law of God that had, in the old days, been given through Moses. There was a concern to learn this so that Israel could return to the old ways from which she had been deviating for so long. It was, apparently, this antiquarian interest that led to a collection and combination of those documents in which the traditions of Israel's past had been set down and in which the law of God for Israel had been preserved.

So it was that the J Document and the E Document came to be combined.[3] One factor in this combination of the two forms of the tradition was the interest of the Palestinian community of the exilic period in finding every witness to Israel's purer past. Another, however, was that same drive toward unity that had long before caused the J Document to collect the traditions of all parts of Israel and to relate them to one another. The sorry remnant of Israel left in Palestine wanted to make it possible for both those to whom the J form of the traditions was best known and those to whom the E form of the traditions was best known to take their place in the new community.

So it was too that Deuteronomy came into being in the form in which it now exists—on the basis of the earlier code or codes that lay behind it. And so it was, probably, that Deuteronomy came to be joined with J and E so that Palestinian Israel had a book in which the traditions by which she was trying to live could be more definitely preserved.

Furthermore, it was probably in the same community that the story of what had happened to Israel after the time of Saul and David was added to the stories (whether separate or part of the combined J and E) now found in I and II Samuel. On the basis of royal chronicles and of temple records and prophetic legends and other accounts, the history of the two kingdoms from the time of Solomon until the destruction of Jerusalem was told. This bringing of Israel's history up to date is now found in I and II Kings. The telling of the history was colored by the point of view of the kingdom outlined above; hence the recurrent judgment that such-and-such a king "did that which was evil in the sight of Yahweh." The kings who escape that judgment can be numbered on the fingers of one hand.[4]

Thus, separated from the leadership of the former ruling house and of the priests connected with that house, the Israelites left in Palestine moved in what was, like the prophetic revolution some three centuries before, essentially a reactionary direction. There was a desire to get back to what Israel *had* been. There was a desire to wipe out the history that had led to the present and to get back to the Israel of Moses' day. It was this desire that led to the combination of J and E and Deuteronomy into a book to which Israel could refer, a further major step in the formation of the Old Testament.[5]

THE EXILIC COMMUNITY

Those Israelites exiled to Babylonia, some at Nebuchadrezzar's first invasion in 597 B.C. and others after the fall of Jerusalem in 587, were adherents of the same faith that motivated those who had been left behind in devastated Palestine.[6] They knew that faith, however, as it had been handed down and interpreted and cultically confessed in Jerusalem. For them it had been through the covenant with David that Yahweh drew near to his people. For them the ordered worship of the temple with its system of sacrifices and its yearly round of festivals and fasts was the means by which Israel remembered her God and proclaimed her loyalty to him. For them the monarchy had not been merely some political system of government. It was the institution that stood behind the whole system of temple worship. The king, the successor of David, was not merely a ruler but also a priest after the order of Melchizedek. Through the presence and the life of the king, in the cult as well as in the more secular phases of life, God held his people together in a unity and imparted to them that blessing in which peace and wholeness were to be found.

When, therefore, an Ezekiel was called out of their midst to prophesy specifically against the king and the temple cultus, and when history bore out the prophecy of Ezekiel, more than a *coup d'état* had affected the exiles. The very structure of their faith had been shaken and collapsed:

> By the waters of Babylon,
> there we sat down and wept,
> when we remembered Zion . . .
> How shall we sing Yahweh's song
> in a foreign land? (Psalm 137:1,4)

The little book Lamentations—traditionally but incorrectly attributed to Jeremiah—gives expression to the same broken spirit.

The prophets who had addressed themselves directly to Jerusalem—Isaiah and Jeremiah and Ezekiel—had all, in effect, to indict the southern kingdom for the same thing. The reason, they said, for the terrible events in which Israel and Jerusalem and the temple were being brought to destruction lay in the fact that Israel had forgotten her vocation to be the people through whose life the sovereignty of the Lord God over history and over the world were to be proclaimed. She had thus forgotten the meaning of her existence. She had ordered her life as if the meaning of her existence were to be found in what she was as a world power, as a national state. This fundamental misconception of what she was had corrupted her very life—and all the structures through which it found expression. That life, therefore, and those structures had to go. That, for the prophets, was the meaning of the Assyrian threat and the coming of the Babylonians.

When, in the exilic community, the prophetic message had been grasped by some and the tragedy that had befallen Israel had been seen to have some meaning in the ongoing purpose of God, the question of Israel's future in God's purpose could be raised as it had been in Palestine. It is quite understandable that the program that began to be laid out for Israel in the exilic community was not unconnected with the program in which, for them, Israel had confessed her faith in her God in the past. What the temple and the ordered worship of the temple cult had meant was not forgotten by the community in which the priests of Jerusalem were leaders. How, deprived of her national structure, does Israel go on being Israel? That was the question for the exilic community.

The answer at which that community gradually arrived was one in which they did not reject all they had known either for a return to the past or for a completely new kind of life. Israel, they said, is the people to whom it has been given to know who God really is. Israel, among all the peoples, is the people with a right knowledge of whom it is that man should worship and of the ways in which he should be worshipped. Israel is that people, among all the peoples, who offer to the true God the worship that is his due. That was why Israel was given a land and became a kingdom. That was why Jerusalem, with its ancient and impressive cult, became the city to which the tribes went up. Therein lay the real meaning of Israel's existence.

To the exilic community, then, the catastrophe which the prophets had insisted was the work of God himself came to be seen as the means by which God was teaching Israel to recognize what was essential in her life. It was not the king, but the cultus in which the king played a large part, that was essential. It was not the palace but the temple that was the real center of Jerusalem. Stripped now by history of her national trappings,

Israel could proceed to be what she was meant to be: the worshipping community through whose prayer and praise the life of the whole world could be related to the God who had created the whole world and to whom it belonged.

The plans laid down by the priests of the exilic community for the life of the new Israel were not manufactured out of whole cloth. The customs and traditions by which the worship of the Jerusalem temple was ordered went back to the cultus that had existed in Jerusalem long before David took that city. They went back also to the faith of Israel and the faith of Judah and to the unity David had wrought of these forms of faith in Yahweh with the ancient faith of Jerusalem. The ways by which Israel was to worship the Lord God, and the ways by which she insured her own holiness for that worship, were to be found in already extant customs well-remembered by the exiled priests.[7]

It is extremely likely that the customs by which the Jerusalem cultus was governed had never been committed to writing—at least not in any systematically organized form. Those customs, which might appear very complicated to an outsider, were so well known by the priests that they were second nature to them. When the modern reader looks at the record of those customs as found in the book of Leviticus, he marvels at their complexity. If, however, he took it upon himself to write out a description of the steps in his own daily routine, he would produce a document just as complicated. The ritual regulations of the Pentateuch are the record of customs known to the Jerusalem priests from time immemorial and passed down from generation to generation. If they are complicated and confused, they are so in the same way that directions given by an "old timer" to a tourist sound complicated and confused to the outsider to whom they are abstractions and not descriptions of well-known concrete movements.

The conviction of the exilic community that history had taught Israel that her vocation was to be the people by whom the one true God should be rightly and truly worshipped led to a new interest in the customs by which the worship of the Jerusalem temple had been governed. That conviction led to a desire to remember those customs, collect them, and compare them with one another.

Obviously it was not possible for the exilic community immediately to put its program for Israel into effect. The full operation of that program required occupation once again of Jerusalem and the rebuilding of the destroyed temple. The customs of the Jerusalem cultus had, however, provided not only for the way in which the worship was to be carried out, but for the way in which the worshippers were to prepare themselves for it. Those customs laid down the steps leading to the ritual cleanliness necessary in the person or the people who were to draw near to the holy God.

When, therefore, it was still impossible for Israel to offer her worship in its fullness because of her separation from Jerusalem, it was, nevertheless, possible for those regulations providing for the ritual cleanliness of Israel to be followed. If history had not, at this point, made it possible for Israel completely to be what she now saw she must be, she could at least hold herself in readiness. She could abide by those provisions for holiness so important to the community in which the one true and holy God was to be properly worshipped. There could, at least, be outward and visible signs of Israel's loyalty to God, signs which would not depend upon the ability, worthiness, or ethical attainments of Israel. There could still be objective given means by which Israel identified herself as the people of God.

Such was the spirit and the desire that lay behind the development, in the exilic community, of emphasis on the three primary marks by which an Israelite could be distinguished wherever he might be: the observance of the Sabbath; the eating of only that meat from which the blood had been drained; and circumcision. These three observances did not originate in

The Witness of the Priestly Synthesis   99

the exile. They had originated so far back in the dim past that no one knew how old they were. They were, to the exiles, as old as Moses, as Abraham, as creation itself. They were, the exilic community came to believe, the signs by which loyalty to God had been confessed from time immemorial. Thus, membership in the Israelite community did not depend upon common adherence to some set of beliefs or upon some subjective religious experience. Neither did it depend (and the isolationist direction taken by later Judaism under the pressure of events tends to obscure this) upon birth. He was an Israelite who observed the Sabbath, who kept the dietary laws, and who was circumcised. Right up until the present time those are the basic marks by which a Jew is known. Whatever culture might surround him, wherever he might be, whatever might be his own personal philosophy or belief, a man was a part of Israel if he did what Israel did.

The conviction that the Israelite community must be the holy community in which the true worship of God was offered found expression in various other exilic developments. That conviction was dominant in the circle in which the career of the prophet Ezekiel was remembered, and the way in which that circle handed down and interpreted Ezekiel's message was colored by it. That conviction found expression also in the collection of the series of provisions for moral and ritual purity known as the Holiness Code (Leviticus 17-26).[8] These writings may sometimes seem to reflect an interest in custom and ritual as ends in themselves; but if they do, it is a distortion of the purpose they were meant to serve. They were meant to indicate concretely, not on the basis of spur-of-the-moment inspiration but on the basis of ancient custom, the ways in which Israel must maintain in herself that holiness becoming a people the end of whose existence was the worship of the holy God.

Yet all this was mere preparation, from the point of view of the leaders of the exilic community, for Israel's principal duty. That duty was the reinstitution of the ordered worship of God in his chosen sanctuary at Jerusalem. The pathetic yearning of those who saw this as the goal of Israel's life is reflected in a number of the Psalms:

> If I forget you, O Jerusalem,
> let my right hand wither!
> Let my tongue cleave to the roof of my mouth,
> if I do not remember you . . . (Psalm 137:5,6)

> Oh send out thy light and thy truth;
> let them lead me,
> let them bring me to thy holy hill
> and to thy dwelling! (Psalm 43:3)

It must be remembered that Second Isaiah originated in the exile, and the interpretation of the coming of Cyrus as the work of God enabling Israel to return to Palestine that is found in Second Isaiah was not unaffected by the dreams for Israel that had developed in the exile. Though Isaiah 40-55 reflects it most profoundly, the joy expressed in those chapters must have been felt at the coming of Cyrus by all to whom the fall of Jerusalem and the prophetic interpretation of it had brought a new vision of what Israel must be.

A GRADUAL RETURN

The steps by which the post-exilic reconstruction came about are veiled in the mists of the past, and any attempt to trace them will be very tentative. It is clear, however, that the dreams of the exiles did not come to immediate fulfillment. In spite of the freedom to return that came with Persian rule, it was hard for Jews who had now lived in Babylonia for fifty or more years to pull up roots and move. A new generation had arisen. Many had no firsthand remembrance of Palestine, and had stakes in property and business in Babylonia. The dreams of the priests and the prophets were all right, but the ordinary Jew could not afford to give up what he had gained

The Witness of the Priestly Synthesis   *101*

in Mesopotamia to start life anew in a devastated and poverty-stricken "old country." [9]

Nevertheless, a few enthusiasts must have begun to trickle into Palestine following the coming of Cyrus in 539 B.C. The tradition preserved in the first six chapters of the book of Ezra has it that a very large group of exiles returned under the leadership of one Sheshbazzar in the year following the coming of Cyrus. That tradition has undoubtedly exaggerated the number, as well as the alacrity, of those who returned. But the first six chapters of Ezra do reflect what was true: that real rebuilding of the temple could not immediately get under way, and that the returnees and the plans they had for what Israel must now become were not met with enthusiasm by those who had remained in the land all along.

Two decades later the temple had still not been rebuilt, and the prophets Haggai and Zechariah had to reprove the people for the lack of fervor which left the dreams of the exiles still unfulfilled. And, even though an appeal to the Persian ruler for help may have resulted in some sort of completion of the temple in 516 B.C. and in the resumption of worship there, the state of the cult and of the city some seventy-five years later in 445 B.C. was such that it could shock Nehemiah, the pious lay adherent of the priestly program for Israel. Only half a century of vigorous effort by Nehemiah and his supporters resulted in any approximation of what the exilic priests and prophets had envisaged as the ideal Israel.[10]

The period of disillusionment that followed the coming of Persian rule was, in some ways, more terrible for Israel than the tragic destruction of an earlier day. The confirmation brought to the prophetic diagnosis of the truth by the downfall of the nation had resulted in a hope that was strong and confident. When that hope remained unfulfilled in spite of the removal of outward restraint, a pathetic depression seized those who had hoped most eagerly. The concentration on self-preservation brought about by poverty, which left no time or energy for attention to the temple; the apathy of those who knew what the prophets had said but did not act on that knowledge; the downright antagonistic attitude of those Israelites who had remained in the land during the period of exile— these were more demoralizing to those who had caught a vision of a new Israel than actual persecution and destruction. The denunciations and encouragements of Isaiah 56-66, of Malachi, and of parts of the other prophetic books were called forth by this period of disillusionment.[11]

Beginning, however, with the coming of Nehemiah to Palestine in the middle of the fifth century B.C., those holding the view of Israel which had come out of the exile took more positive steps to insure the accomplishment of their program. It may be that that program, based as it was on the customs and regulations of the cult of Jerusalem and on the myths and legends in which those customs and regulations were accounted for, had already begun to be committed to writing earlier. Certainly, the Holiness Code of Leviticus 17-26 must already have been written down. Now, however, there was a concentrated effort to have down in a definite way what Israel was to be and to do as the holy people of the holy God.

Undoubtedly one of the reasons for this move to commit to writing the theology and practice of Israel, as the exilic party saw them, lay in the opposition of those Israelites who had remained in Palestine all along. The latter had, as indicated above, adopted the view of Israel taken in the E Document and in Deuteronomy. They were certain that it was her becoming a kingdom that had resulted in the disaster through which Israel had passed. They were suspicious of anything that might be associated with kingship, and this, as well as their fear of Persian displeasure at any appearance of nationalism among the Jews, lay behind their opposition to any rebuilding of the former capital or its temple. Furthermore, they were in possession of a book in which the ancient traditions of Israel were preserved—the combination of J, E, and Deuteronomy—and those traditions quite clearly supported their view of the matter. It is true that the J Document with its theology and its more favorable view of kingship was part of their book, but its combination with the laws of E and Deuteronomy tended to make what it was saying hard to discern.[12]

To the priestly party—such is an appropriate designation of those who maintained the idea of Israel that had been preserved in the exile—the point of view taken by their opponents misinterpreted the nature of Israel's vocation. Yes, the lesson of history as enunciated by the prophets had been that the Israelite monarchy had to go in order that Israel might discern her true destiny. But to forgo along with national ambition the cult of Jerusalem and all that it represented was to throw out the baby with the bath water—in spite of what the sacred book of the Palestinian Israelites might say. Behind the faith of the priestly party lay a tradition equally as old as that embodied in the book of their opponents. That tradition was not so inseparably connected with monarchy that what it really embodied could not survive the collapse of monarchy. Its seeds lay in the ancient faith of Israel that went back to Moses, back to the patriarchs, back to the very beginning of the world.

THE PRIESTLY CODE

The strand in the Old Testament known as the Priestly Code came into existence in order to express the more positive steps taken by the priestly party after the coming of Nehemiah, as well as to voice opposition to the view of the Palestinian party. Though the situation in Palestine in the fifth century B.C. gave rise to its formal compilation, the code embodied the ancient regulations of the Jerusalem cult and the traditions of Israel as they had been preserved and handed down in Jerusalem for long ages.

Though the Priestly Code is basically a manual of regulations for the worship of the Israelite community, it is, in typically Hebraic fashion, cast into the form of a narrative. This is owing, to some extent, to the desire of the compilers to show that the view of Israel embodied in the code is related to the ancient history of their people. But, more profoundly, it is due to the basic nature of Israelite faith, whatever interpretation might be put upon it, as a faith that had its roots in history.

The narrative of the Priestly Code, however, is always subservient to theology and to the explanation and specification of Israel's obligations as the people called to worship the one true God. Indeed, this reflects the way in which, for the Priestly Code, history is subservient to the purpose for which God had called Israel into being. Unlike the J Document, which definitely has a point of view in accord with which its recounting of history is organized and yet which is interested in the account for its own sake, the Priestly Code is more interested in its own view of the meaning of history than it is in the history from which that view has come. Thus, the only places at which the Priestly Code pauses to indulge in any extensive narrative are those at which the narrative is explanatory of some important part of the system in accord with which Israel's cult is organized. Otherwise the Priestly Code summarizes history and makes the necessary connections by means of genealogical summaries. The "begats" of the Old Testament narrative are the work of the compilers of the Priestly Code, although they probably go back to very ancient tradition.

The outline of the Priestly Code is quite simple. The four chief parts of that outline take the form of stages in God's dealing with his world: four successive covenants in which the obligations being fulfilled by Israel for all the world have been laid upon men.[13]

Though the word *covenant* is not applied to it in the Priestly Code, the first step in the plan of God was creation. The majestic account of God's calling of the universe into being found in the opening chapter of Genesis was the beginning of the Priestly Code. As had the J Document long before, the Priestly Code drew upon traditions of creation common to the ancient Near East. Indeed, the creation story of the Priestly Code may very well have been part of the tradition of the Jerusalem cultus for a long time before the exile, going back to the connections of that ancient city with the culture and religion of the world of which it was a part.

Like the J creation story, the priestly account of creation serves to relate the history of Israel to the history of the whole world, and to assert that the God with whose purpose the fortunes of Israel have been bound up is the God of the whole world. But, more than that, it specifically relates the obligations fulfilled by Israel as a worshipping community to the nature of the created order: "On the seventh day, God rested and blessed and hallowed the seventh day." Thus does the Priestly Code assert that the Sabbath which is of obligation to Israel is not some merely religious observance of one particular people. It is a part of the very structure of the universe. When Israel observes the Sabbath, it is not fulfilling some merely religious duty. It is behaving, as all men should, in accord with the nature of things as they are—in accord with the purpose of the Creator of all things. In the observance of the Sabbath by Israel, creation itself takes pleasure.

The Priestly Code links the creation story with the account of the great flood by genealogies. Again, the purpose of the Priestly Code in the account of Noah and the flood is more than the connection, after the fashion of J, of Israel's story with universal history. In P the climax of the flood story comes in the covenant God makes between himself and mankind, and of his promise to spare mankind from any further destruction the rainbow is the perpetual sign. Of the obligation of man under that covenant to honor life, the draining of the blood—which was to ancient man the seat of life—from slaughtered animals was to be the sign. Thus, once again, the ritual observances of Israel—this time the basic dietary laws—are interpreted not simply as religious rites peculiar to one people. The covenant with Noah, in the scheme of the Priestly Code, was made before Israel existed. It was a covenant with mankind as a whole. The dietary laws observed by Israel, therefore, are part of the given framework of all human life. In the performance of them Israel is acting on behalf of all men. Once again the point is made that the purpose of Israel is to be the worshipping community, set in the midst of the world, through whom human life is rightly related to the one true God from whom it came and to whom it belongs.

Again, genealogies are employed by the Priestly Code to connect the time of Noah with the time of Abraham. And, in its account of Abraham, the Priestly Code concentrates once more on the institution of one of the basic practices in Israel's cultic tradition—circumcision. The Sabbath had been ordained as the sign of the covenant of God with his whole creation. The rainbow and the ban on the eating of blood had been made the signs of God's covenant with all mankind. Now circumcision is the sign of the covenant with Abraham and his seed. Thus the successive covenants, of which the distinctive rites of Israel are signs, represent a process of increasing concentration in which God is drawing nearer and nearer to a particular people. They represent an unfolding of the purpose of God in which he was working, beginning with creation and continuing through successive ages, toward the calling of a people by whom the worship due him might be offered. The covenant with Abraham, with its sign of circumcision, brings the purpose one step closer to accomplishment.

There is very little real narrative in the Priestly Code between Abraham and Moses, for the next and climactic step in the working out of God's plan took place, according to P, with Moses. Characteristically, the narrative in which Moses figures has to do with the institution of matters connected with Israel's worship of God. Like the E Document, the Priestly Code says that it was only with Moses that men began to call God by his proper name. The Priestly Code, however, claims that more than the true name and nature of God were revealed to Moses. To him was given the right and complete knowledge of the way in which men should worship the one true God. It was with that knowledge that the law given by Moses had really to do.

It is the Priestly Code that dwells on the role of Aaron as priest, that gives attention to the regulations for the Passover and the feast of Unleavened Bread in connection with the exodus and then—in most of Exodus 25 through Numbers 10:28—sets down in detail the regulations for Israel's worship. Those regulations were the most important part of the law given to Moses at the holy mountain according to the Priestly Code. Thus it is with this fourth stage in its schematic history—the covenant with Moses—that the Priestly Code arrives at its climax. Contrary to stories in the J and E Documents, the Priestly Code studiously avoids any mention of sacrifice before the time of Moses. Only according to the regulations given through Moses, only through the priesthood (Aaron and the Levites) authorized by Moses, only under the covenant sealed with Israel through the mediation of Moses, could the one true God be properly worshipped. This is what the Priestly Code was saying in the middle of the fifth century B.C. when Israel was disillusioned and apathetic and divided: the *raison d'être* of Israel is the proper worship of the holy God as provided for in the Mosaic covenant—this and nothing else.

Those portions of the Pentateuch which come from the Priestly Code provide some of the most boring reading in the Bible. The modern reader must remember, however, that they were not intended to be thrilling reading, to be inspirational in any individualistic or sentimental sense. They were intended to be the handbook by which the Israelite community ordered its worship of God and to provide a justification for that worship.

The conception that stands behind them is a grand one. They are the spelling out of a great vision of the vocation of Israel.

THE FINAL SYNTHESIS

Although our only information comes from reading between the lines, the vigorous effort of the priestly party, beginning with Nehemiah, out of which the Priestly Code came, seems to have been unable either to convince the Palestinian Israelites of the validity of the priestly position or to accomplish its aims without their support. The obstacles to a unified Israel were undoubtedly connected with personalities and issues in the immediate situation of the fifth century B.C., but they found their roots in the old differences between the sons of Israel and the house of Judah, between Shechem and Jerusalem, between north and south. The priestly party would not accept the validity of the conception of Israel found in the Palestinian party's J-E-Deuteronomy, nor would the Palestinian party accept the Priestly Code.

The result of all this was that in the fifth century, as five centuries earlier in the time of David, some kind of accommodation of the two traditions to one another had to take place if Israel was to be a unity. In the compromise of the fifth century B.C.—as in the previous age of David—Jerusalem became the center of the life of the community while those who had the most stake in Jerusalem accepted a good deal of the theology of the group from outside Jerusalem. The priestly party's vision of Israel as the holy people whose whole life was directed toward the offering of proper worship to the one true God in his sanctuary at Jerusalem became reality. The theology of the Palestinian party, however, with its insistence on the uniqueness of the faith of Israel and on the impossibility of any compromise of that faith found an important and prominent place in the settlement.

The literary result of this *rapprochement* of the fifth century was the completion of the Pentateuch as we know it today. The book of the Palestinian party (J-E-Deuteronomy) was combined with the Priestly Code so as to produce Genesis, Exodus, Leviticus, Numbers, and Deuteronomy in practically their present form. The birth of the Pentateuch out of this compromise represented a seeming victory for the priestly party, for the Priestly Code provided the framework into which the other elements were put. In the finished Pentateuch, it is the great, schematic plan of the Priestly Code into which the traditions and laws from the J Document, the E Document, and Deuteronomy were fitted. It is the creation story of the Priestly Code with which the finished Pentateuch begins. It is the Priestly Code's account of the Noachian covenant (Genesis 9) that is the climax of the story of the great flood. The Priestly Code's treatment of the institution and importance of circumcision occupies an important place in the stories concerning Abraham (Genesis 17). In the account of Moses, the exodus, and the sojourn at the holy mountain, the provisions of the Priestly Code for the worship of Israel are so numerous and so detailed that they swamp the narrative of the J Document and the laws of the E Document. And the legislation of Deuteronomy, in which the northern position is so strikingly put, is attached only as an appendix to the end of the Pentateuch, the relation of it to the priestly legislation being indicated by its very name—the "second law." [14]

Not only did the point of view of the priestly party predominate in the compilation of the Pentateuch, but other parts of the growing body of literature that was to become the Old Testament were edited and altered in accord with the doctrine of the centrality of Jerusalem to which the Palestinian party had to accede in the compromise that brought Israel together. For example, an attempt was made to edit the book that had grown out of the ministry of the prophet Hosea in the northern kingdom so as to make it appear that he had addressed himself to the south. A detailed account of the dedication of the temple by Solomon—to cite another example—was put into the history of the kingdoms that had been compiled from the theological point of view of E and Deuteronomy (I Kings 6-8). Again, the story of the reform in 621 B.C., in which King Josiah had proclaimed his independence of Assyria, was elaborated to make it appear that Deuteronomy had not come from the north but had been found in the temple at Jerusalem (II Kings 22-23).[15]

The reason for the predominance of the point of view of the priestly party in the post-exilic settlement is probably twofold. In the first place, that party developed a well-defined and aggressive program which, apparently, was approved of, and supported by, the Persian Empire. It easily prevailed over the essentially reactionary temper of the Palestinian party, and must have persuaded some members of the latter group to give their free consent to it. Secondly, that program had the backing of the comparatively wealthy and increasingly influential Jewish community in Babylonia. It was from that community that financial support and spiritual and intellectual leadership came through many centuries.[16]

The priestly party, however, had won a Pyrrhic victory. The "publication" of an official book into which the points of view, as well as the forms of words held dear by both sides in the controversy, were put did not heal all the differences by which Israel was divided. The community the priests had sought to bring together proved to be less lasting than the book compiled to produce it. At some point, members of the Palestinian party who were not satisfied with the domination of things by the Jerusalem priests broke away and built their own temple on Mount Gerazim, hard by the site of ancient Shechem. Thus did the Samaritans come to be permanently separated from the Jews. It was bitter religious controversy that led to the hatred and contempt with which the Jews of New Testament times regarded the Samaritans. But the schism must have taken place after the formation of the Pentateuch, for the Samaritans still possess it in the same form as the Jews.[17]

It was the Samaritan schism that prompted some rabid adherent of the priestly party to write a history of Israel from the beginning of the world up until the time of Nehemiah and Ezra. This writer obviously drew on other writings, notably the books of Samuel and Kings, for his material. His narrative neither improves upon that of the books from Genesis to Kings, nor contributes much information not found in those books. It is chiefly noted for the way in which it ignores, as far as possible, the north and the northern kingdom and takes the view that the whole tradition that lay behind the Samaritan schism never existed. It is marked also by a devoted interest in the cult of the post-exilic temple at Jerusalem. The work of this writer, the Chronicler, is found in I and II Chronicles, Ezra and Nehemiah—all of which were once a single work.[18]

More, however, than the outward fact of the Samaritan schism and the unrest that led to it shattered the priestly party's vision of the form life in post-exilic Israel should take. The Priestly Code with its concept of Israel as the community which had discerned its vocation to offer the worship properly prescribed for the true God may have been the basis of the Pentateuch. The historical books may have been edited to emphasize the importance and centrality of Jerusalem and the temple. Yet, the very fact that, in opposition to the claims that the Palestinian party had made for its book, the priestly party had first to give its own program for Israel written form, and then to combine its document with the other in order to find a basis of agreement, created an interest in the book as such. This interest resulted in the book in which the program was spelled out coming to have as much prestige as the program itself.

Such a development of the religion of the book ensued that, when the temple was destroyed by the Romans in A.D. 70 and the system of worship outlined in the Pentateuch could no longer be practiced, Judaism could survive, comparatively unaffected. The synagogue—the gathering in which the book was read and studied—replaced the temple as the center of Jewish life even before the temple was destroyed. Though the priestly party had won out so far as the form was concerned, the Palestinian party had won in terms of the character of Judaism. It was neither the historically oriented faith of the J Document and the prophets nor the priestly view of Israel as the holy people worshipping the holy God in ancient and splendid forms, but the view of the E Document and Deuteronomy in which Israel was defined in terms of a past recorded in a book that came to be predominant.

The emphasis upon an authoritative book that produced the Pentateuch was also responsible for a tendency toward definition of authoritativeness in other areas. The collections of sayings, stories, and interpretations that had grown out of the careers of the great prophets came to be set down in definitely circumscribed books. Just as the literary form of the law had been definitely set down in the Pentateuch, there came into being a canon of the prophets. In the Hebrew Bible the latter includes the former prophets (the books from Joshua through II Kings with the exception of Ruth) and the latter prophets (the books from Isaiah to the end of the English Old Testament with the exception of Lamentations and Daniel). Further, the songs in which Israel had from ancient times praised her God came to be collected into a definite book, the Psalter,[19] which was divided, in imitation of the Pentateuch, into five books. The tendency toward a religion of the book had affected every phase of Israel's life.

The result of this development was that neither prophecy nor any of the other means by which Israel had discerned God at work in history in the past was any longer a live thing. They had become institutionalized, defined in terms of the contents of certain recognized books. Both the narrative in which the J Document had witnessed to the sovereignty of God and the pronouncements in which the great prophets had done the same thing had been given a religious status and associated with an orthodoxy. Thus the ongoing movement of history—of which the Samaritan schism and the rise of Alexander the Great were instances—was no longer taken account of in any vital way. The victory of the religion of a closed book with its orientation toward the past, and the development of a closed orthodoxy through which, it must be admitted, the ancient Israelite faith was transmitted in hard times, made it necessary for witness to the sovereignty of the living God to take new and unaccustomed forms.

CHAPTER FIVE

Later Attempts to Witness

Given the fact that the Old Testament as a book is, in its final form, the sacred scripture of a religious community, the amount of material included in it in which the official dogmas of that community are criticized is remarkable. Even that tendency toward a religion of the book, in which latter day inspiration and workings of God's spirit were not allowed for, could not shut out the prophetic spirit. That spirit might have to find new forms in which to express itself, but its objection to any attempt to deny that lordship of Israel's God to which the J Document and the prophets had borne witness continued to be expressed. Attempts to absolutize systems or institutions, to invest them with the authority that belonged to God alone, were ridiculed and resisted.

In spite of the universalism of the Priestly Code, resistance to efforts of the exilic party to reestablish the cult at Jerusalem and apathy within the Jewish community itself led to a rigorism and an exclusiveness compatible neither with that universalism nor with the humane tone of Deuteronomy. In order to keep the holy people from losing its identity, Nehemiah and Ezra had not only to legislate against marriages between Jews and foreigners, but even to force Jews to put away foreign wives to whom they were already married.[1] The conviction that Israel was the people chosen by the one true God to be his witnesses in the world could and did lead to self-satisfaction and pride, and these attitudes were only aggravated by the indifference and hostility with which the Jews were regarded by other peoples. A good many of the passages in the prophetic books in which foreign nations are so scathingly denounced bear witness not only to the prophetic faith in the universality of God's righteous sovereignty but also to Jewish prejudice.[2] As Nahum could, in the seventh century B.C., gleefully celebrate the fall of the Assyrian capital Nineveh, so Obadiah could, in post-exilic times, gloat over the collapse of the Edomites at the advance of the Arabs into the area southeast of Palestine. And the book of Esther—admitted to the canon because of its claim to explain the origins of the feast of Purim—is evidence of the growth of a narrow, bitter nationalism.[3]

Two of the most exquisite books in the Old Testament come from the post-exilic period, and direct a gentle, even humorous, rebuke to the spirit of exclusiveness and rigorism by which the community was coming to be characterized. The book of Ruth takes the form of a romantic idyll, set in the days before the kingdom of Saul and David came into being. Its heroine is a young woman whose faithfulness to the family of her deceased husband and to her destitute mother-in-law is above and beyond that demanded by law and custom. The story reaches a conclusion in which the heroine's virtue and devotion are rewarded with a second marriage of which love and happiness and wealth are parts.

Though the tale of Ruth may be based on an older story, its present form was contrived to bring a subtle message to the fifth-century Jewish community. The heroine, so faithful to the Israelite family and community into which she had married, was a foreigner, a Moabitess. No one would have missed this point when Nehemiah had forced Jews to put away their foreign wives. Furthermore, the genealogy with which the book ends quietly makes the point that this faithful Moabitess became the great grandmother of David. Thus, in the tradition of the Court Chronicle and the J Document, without pietism or moralism, an objection is made to the system in which post-exilic Israel was trying to enclose the activity of the living God.[4]

The book of Jonah comes from this same general period, and makes the same point. Even though the author has made an ancient prophet, mentioned in II Kings 14:25, the hero of his story, the book is pure fiction. Jonah is sent by God to exhort the inhabitants of Nineveh, the Assyrian capital, to repent. In spite of the fact that when Jonah was written, the Assyrian empire had been defunct for two centuries at least, it was still remembered in Israel as a terrible and ruthless power. The post-exilic readers would have understood the reluctance of the ancient prophet to embark upon such a hopeless mission as that of preaching repentance to Nineveh. Yet, the writer insists, that was just what God wanted, and so constant was his purpose that the prophet could not escape. Moreover, when the result of Jonah's preaching was that Nineveh did repent, God—and this was even more incredible to post-exilic exclusivism—pardoned that city. So the pouting Jonah at the conclusion of the book mirrors the attitude of Israel in the author's time, and the rebuke of God to the prophet is a rebuke to the author's contemporaries. Again, the humor, the restraint, the lack of moralism, are worthy of the tradition that began with the J Document.[5]

THE WISDOM LITERATURE

Ruth and Jonah are isolated examples of why it was impossible for the community which preserved the J Document and the words of the prophets ever completely to become a reactionary religious sect. Yet the fact that the very vehicles through which witness in the past had been given to the sovereignty of the living God were now institutionalized made it difficult for either historical narrative or prophetic pronouncement to continue in the great tradition.

The narrative in which the J writer had proclaimed his faith in a God known through his unfolding purpose in history was now part of an official, sacrosanct book. The words in which the prophets had seen world-shaking events as judgments of the Lord God of all things were now also preserved in sacred books or venerable traditions. The prophetic conviction that the righteous sovereignty of God explained the course of events had been married to the covenant theology of the E Document and Deuteronomy, and reduced to the neat formulas by which the rulers of Israel and Judah are summarily praised or condemned by the editors of the books of the Kings. So both narrative and prophecy were the property of the official religion, and voices of protest had, of necessity, to find other vehicles through which they could speak. Even Ruth and Jonah, ostensibly narrative and prophecy, were really parodies. This development is the background against which the theological role of the wisdom literature of the Old Testament is to be understood.

The wisdom movement as such did not originate in postexilic times. Indeed, it had existed before ever the J Document was put into writing. Its origins are so old as to be irrecoverable, and it was honored at the court of every kingdom of the ancient Near East. When, under Solomon, Israel built the buildings, developed the institutions, and made the contacts that went with being a real kingdom, wise men came to be associated with the royal court. It is undoubtedly for this reason that Solomon came to be thought of as the wise man *par excellence*—just as David, in whose reign the psalmody connected with the Jerusalem cult came to be important in Israel, was considered to be the psalmist *par excellence*.[6]

The wise men were, basically, the civil service of the court. They were the custodians of the art of writing, and were responsible for the royal correspondence and the royal records.

Furthermore, they were the mediators of international culture and probably delighted in collecting and passing along what was good in the literature and song of the nations with which they came into contact. They were the mentors of the king and of his entourage in the ways of the world. The nature of their position and their contacts undoubtedly kept them from putting their roots down too deeply into one national culture or religion. They might have appreciated the art of the Court Chronicle or the J Document—though they would have refrained from commitment to the faith behind those writings—but they would have considered the temper of the tradition behind the E Document and Deuteronomy to be naive and rather grossly credulous. The obvious lack of sympathy and understanding with which Rehoboam went to Shechem to hear the demands of the sons of Israel after the death of Solomon may have come, in part at least, from his training at the hands of the wise men of his father's court.[7]

The wise men, then, were suave, worldly, cosmopolitan. They were not prone to delight in the passionate commitment of the man of faith, but in the well-turned phrase, in the balanced poetic couplet, in the pithy aphorism. The form of words in which their art was most characteristically expressed was the *mashal*. Usually translated "proverb," the broader meaning of this word is indicated by the fact that it has sometimes to be translated "riddle" or "by-word," "parable" or "allegory." The *mashal* was a saying in which profundity of thought, keenness of observation, beauty of vocabulary and style, were combined in the service of human wisdom with regard to life and all that made it up. The consideration of some problem or situation by a circle of wise men might result in a saying in which someone summed up the wisdom that had been brought to bear on the matter at hand. That saying might then be repeated and polished in the group. Delight would be taken both in its wisdom and in its beauty of expression.[8]

The profound difference between the Hebraic and the Hellenic minds is indicated by the fact that the wise men did not indulge in theoretical speculation about being and existence. Their concern was with action, with the ethical sphere, with what was sensible, productive, and subject to reward in human life. If they came to the conclusion, as did the editors of the books of the Kings, that good was rewarded and evil punished, they did so from no systematic application of a theological principle. Theirs was a common sense, prudential ethic, interested in results—not in the reason for the results.

That the wise men occupied an honored and responsible place in Israel is indicated by passing references such as that in Jeremiah 18:18, which mentions them along with the priests and the prophets as leaders of the people. They were not, however, particularly influential in the development of the peculiarly Hebraic point of view as it came to be enunciated in the narrative and legal and prophetic parts of the Old Testament. So far as the distinctive biblical faith was concerned, theirs was not a formative role. They were counselors to king and people, but on a more "secular" level. That they preserved and gathered together their wise and beautiful sayings is indicated by the fact that behind the book of Proverbs—which, as a book, comes from post-exilic times—lies a number of older collections.[9]

Though it had had a long and honorable history, it was only in the post-exilic period that the wisdom movement began to play an important theological role. In the age in which Israel's faith was coming to be more and more defined in terms of an official orthodoxy, some new vehicle had to be found through which the spirit of the J Document and of the prophetic movement could find expression. Since the latter had become part of the official system, the wisdom movement provided a means through which witness could still be borne to the mystery and largeness of God and of his purpose. When the theological heritage of Israel had been reduced to a hardened system of doctrine and practice, the humanistic heritage of the wisdom movement became the ground on which a protest was lodged —a protest which was, if sometimes almost sheerly negative, close to a confession of faith.[10]

Though the theological significance of the wisdom literature lies in the open-mindedness that it maintained in the period after the exile, its opposition to strict and rigorous orthodoxy did not always take the form of a direct protest. It was more the direction taken by its thought and the frame of reference in which that thought took place that acted as correctives to the hardening of the more distinctive Hebraic point of view into a closed system.

However much the temper and outlook of the J Document might have differed from those of the E Document and Deuteronomy, and however much the priestly party might have differed from the Palestinian party, there were certain things in the literature that came to form the canon of the law and the canon of the prophets in which the various strands of that literature all shared. For them all, each in its own way, God was the center of attention, and the realm of history was the area in which the self-revelation of God was discerned. Even though the J Document and the Priestly Code might make a great deal of the relation of the story of Israel to the whole world, the orientation of their thought was basically theological and historical. Even though Second Isaiah might make a good deal of the role of Israel's God as the creator of the ends of the earth, the whole argument was based on the conviction that only in terms of the revealed purpose of Israel's God could the course of history be explained.

When, however, in the post-exilic age, the point of view of the narrative and prophetic parts of the Old Testament had come to be associated with a closed orthodoxy, the basic categories of thought behind those types of literature came to be associated with that orthodoxy. There tended to be more and more of an assumption that God had revealed all that there was for man to know about him, and that the historical revelation which had been the basis of Israel's faith was now complete. There was, in other words, no more to be said. Formulas were now available to cover every situation. Later Jewish tradition came to have it that if only one man in Israel would keep the revealed law for one day the kingdom of God would come.

To those who were not content with the assumption that there was no more room or need for consideration of the ultimate questions about life—who were still struck by the mystery of existence—other categories than those of covenant and historical revelation had to be found. Concepts still free to hold largeness and mystery had to be employed if human thought was to do justice to reality. It was just here that the wisdom movement came to exert a great influence in Israel—not only among the wise men themselves, but among others also for whom theological thinking had reached a *cul de sac* in the older terms.

The point is not that the wisdom movement is humanistic as opposed to the more theologically centered strands of the Old Testament. No line was ever drawn by the ancient Israelite between the secular and the sacred spheres. Though, for the sake of convenience, it may be found helpful to distinguish between these two spheres, we must never forget that God was as given a reality to the wise men of ancient Israel as he was to the prophets. The point is that the ways in which the wisdom movement operated and the things to which it directed its attention were not in the control of the formulators of orthodoxy. It is for this reason that the gnomic, parabolic style of the wise men came to be utilized in theological thinking. It is also for this reason that attention was turned more to those things about which human wisdom might be thought capable of drawing some conclusions.

For these reasons emphasis came to be laid more upon man and what was prudent and profitable and sensible for him than upon God and his workings in history. Emphasis came to be laid more upon those abiding principles of human nature and conduct that obtained in any age or situation than upon the particular and unique and once-and-for-all quality of historical events. And, finally, attention came to be directed more toward the constancy and wonder of the natural realm than toward the realm of history. Any speculation about the latter might come into conflict with the dogmatic principles by which the editors of Kings or the Chronicler had organized past history, but the former was a realm in which power and mystery could still bespeak the wonder of God and his ways.

So it was that the wisdom movement in post-exilic Israel did not, at first, voice a direct protest against the orthodoxy which had come to be dominant. Neither did it deny that awareness of the reality and lordship of God in history which had ever been part of the Israelite point of view. It did, however, direct its attention toward ways of thinking and objects of thought not yet hedged about by the regulations of a closed system. It could thus attract the attention of those who had no conscious purpose of revolt, but who could no longer find objects of vital interest in the spheres covered by orthodoxy. Reverence for God was one of its primary characteristics. Indeed, that reverence made those who turned to it dissatisfied with orthodoxy. The fear of the Lord, it held, was alone the beginning of wisdom.

It was apparently this kind of interest in the wisdom movement in the post-exilic age that resulted in the collection of examples of the *mashal* in which the wise men of old had put the truth about man and what was wise for him as they saw it. A new respect for Solomon, the legendary prototype of the Israelite wise man, was born. The basis of the finished book of Proverbs is a collection entitled "The Proverbs of Solomon" (Proverbs 10:1—22:16). The recovery or collection of this booklet probably took place early in the period of renewed interest in wisdom. Its contents are characterized by that common sense, prudential ethic of the wise men of earlier times.

Further "Proverbs of Solomon," in a collection "which the men of Hezekiah King of Judah copied out," were also collected (Proverbs 25-29). A collection which, given its similarity to the "Instruction of Amen-em-Opet," must have originated with Egyptian wise men came into being (Proverbs 22:17—24:22). The words of other foreign wise men, Agur and Lemuel, were also treasured (Proverbs 30-31).

The interest of the wisdom movement in the ways and writings of other peoples and in beauty for its own sake probably also lies behind the collection of such a series of poems as that now known as the Song of Songs.[11] Those poems may have originally been simply love songs, or they may have come from some non-Israelite cult in which a ritual marriage of the king played a part. They probably came to be preserved in Israel in the circles of wise men who were interested in culture for its own sake. The prestige of the wisdom movement which had preserved them, plus the allegorical interpretation later put upon them, finally led to their inclusion in the scriptures. The wise men were also interested in Israel's own poetry, and the tone of the Psalter indicates that they had—in the post-exilic period—a hand in the collection of Hebrew poems found there, even though the origin of the collection is to be sought in the cult of Jerusalem.[12]

Interest in the wise men's more open approach to life led to more than the collecting of their sayings and writings. It led to the conviction, on the part of some, that it was really by the insights of the wisdom movement that the world itself was to be explained. For those whose enthusiasm for the wisdom approach was strongest, the meaning of life could not be most adequately expressed by the covenant or history. It was wisdom which discerned the fundamental principles by which the natural order functioned. Furthermore, it was by wisdom that man could order his life in accord with those principles.

The wisdom movement came, then, to have a theology of its own. When the book of Proverbs was put together in its present form, that theology found expression in the midst of the various collections of which the book was made up. Particularly in the eighth chapter of Proverbs does this theology find expression. There it is not only asserted that wisdom is the fundamental principle by which alone everything that is is to be explained, but wisdom is personified and thought of as the companion of God even before the created universe came into being. It was through wisdom that the heavens and the earth and all things in them were created. It was, therefore, only as wisdom was allowed to speak to the mind of man that man could understand the world of which he was a part and the principles by which God ordered that world.

The effect of the interest of the wisdom movement in creation and in the principles behind it, as well as in the definition of man in terms of his place in creation rather than in those of some particular national tradition, was a universality that called Israel back from the exclusiveness resulting from too narrow a concentration on Israel's particular vocation. Wisdom, thus, though it did not find its origin in those aspects of Israel's life that were distinctively her own, provided a corrective to the restricted view that might result from attentiveness solely to covenant and law. The greatness of the J Document lay in the profundity with which it had not only discerned the distinctiveness of Israel's faith but had also related that faith to the whole of history and creation. When orthodoxy's emphasis on the faith alone had tended to distort the relevance that J had claimed for the faith to life and history, wisdom was the means by which the neglected side of J was given expression. What had, however, been joined together in J had, in the post-exilic period, been put asunder; the moralistic orthodoxy of the editors of the books of Kings made the history of Israel a narrowly religious event; the broader appeal of the wise men tended to lose sight of the historically oriented point of view of J and the prophets.

Though the post-exilic interest in wisdom provided a corrective to overconcentration on covenant and law, it was the law which absorbed the wisdom movement and not vice versa. Just as the religion of the book, of the legalized torah, had taken up into itself the prophetic and priestly movements, so it took up into itself the wisdom movement. Wisdom, too, became institutionalized, became part of the orthodox system, and the pious could use it to express greater devotion to the law. Indeed, personified wisdom and the law—torah—came to be identified so that, in later Judaism, it was not just the fear of the Lord that was the beginning of wisdom, but the law and its observance.[13]

The piety in which this marriage took place finds expression in such things as Psalms 1 and 119. Particularly the latter is expressive of a "torah mysticism" that resulted from the identification of personified wisdom with torah, and the spirit expressed in Psalm 119 had a great deal to do with the final compilation and editing of the psalms. Though their ultimate origin is to be sought in the poetry associated with the cult of Jerusalem, and though it was probably the interest of the post-exilic priestly party in the resumption of that cult that began the collection of the psalms, the present form of the Psalter is that of a manual of private devotion in which the piety resulting from a combination of the ideals of wisdom and of the law predominates.[14]

This same piety lies behind the apocryphal Wisdom of Jesus ben Sirach, commonly called Ecclesiasticus. In the apocryphal Wisdom of Solomon the personified wisdom-torah could be thought of in such a way as to be capable of equation with the logos of Greek thought, and such an equation—with the prophetic concept of the word also having some influence—lies behind the interpretation of Jesus given in the first chapter of John. It was this absorption of all that wisdom meant into the law—the tradition that had come from the old northern confederation through the E Document and Deuteronomy—

that resulted in the characteristically wise, reverent, and philosophical Jewish respect for torah.

The gradual absorption of the wisdom movement into the system against which it had provided a corrective did not, however, take place without protest. There were those who saw clearly the issue that most adherents of the wisdom movement had only felt. Their objection to any neat orthodoxy which, in terms of covenant or wisdom or whatever, presumed to define the ways of God found expression in two writings: Job and Ecclesiastes.

Though they are protesting against the direction that orthodox wisdom was taking, Job and Ecclesiastes do so from within the tradition of the wisdom movement. Theirs is not the kind of objection to the wise men that an Elijah might have raised. In the same kind of exalted and polished language, in the same probing and questioning ways employed by the wise men from ancient times, the authors of Job and Ecclesiastes voice their protest against any attempt to contain God and his ways within the precepts of a system.

The close connections of the book of Job with the wisdom movement are manifest in the way in which that book obviously came into being over a considerable period of time.[15] It is the result of the probing of one particular theme by various authors who expressed their probings in the most polished style and language. The process by which the book reached its final form was very much like the process by which a *mashal* would be repeated and improved upon and handed down until it was recorded in a collection like the book of Proverbs.

The book of Job originated in the story of a man whose righteousness was legendary. This story was very well-known, and much older than the age in which the book reached its final form. When, for example, the writer of Ezekiel 14:12 ff. wants to name three men who will be unmistakably accounted righteous by his readers, Job is included among them. The original story of Job, the epitome of the upright man, probably provided some of the details of the opening chapters of the present book. Just what its point was it is not now possible to know because of the use of the figure of Job made by later members of the wisdom movement.

While the prose story with which the book opens leaves the impression that the story has to do with a righteous man whom God tests, and thus implies at its outset a solution to the problem of human suffering, it is in the dialogue between Job and his three friends, cast in the form of dramatic poetry of the highest quality, that the heart of the book lies.[16]

In the dialogue, the basic problem of the book is set forth. Job is a man whose righteousness cannot be doubted. His three friends represent orthodoxy, apparently orthodoxy of the sort that came of the absorption of the wisdom ethic into the covenant and law theology. The orthodox position was that, due both to the covenant under which Israel lived and to the principles undergirding creation, good must be rewarded in this life and evil punished. Job's contention, given his own suffering in spite of his righteousness, is that this is not true. He will not concede the validity of the orthodox position, be it stated by the kind and wise Eliphaz, who counsels him to hold on and wait for the comfort of God; or by the offended Bildad, who reproves Job for disregarding the knowledge of God that has come from the insights of wisdom; or by the sarcastic Zophar, who explicitly accuses Job of some terrible secret sin which is the cause of his suffering.

Thus in the dialogue, the predicament of Job, the righteous man whose integrity is such that he will not admit guilt or ignorance when he is honestly convinced that they are not present in him, directly refutes the presumptuousness of an orthodoxy claiming to have a definitive knowledge of God and of the laws by which life is governed. The conclusion of the dialogue is a magnificently pathetic statement of Job in which he refuses to accept the arguments of the friends, and directly challenges God to answer him (Job 26:1—27:6; 31). The clear implication of this speech is that there is no meaning to human suffering and that the neat righteousness claimed for God by his orthodox devotees is by no means apparent in human history in the easy way that they claim.

It may very well be that the poetic dialogue once stood by itself. Coming to no conclusion, employing the kind of eloquent restraint used in the conclusion to the book of Jonah, the author was content to sketch vividly the misery by which human life is always attended and to show the bankruptcy of the orthodox answers to the mystery posed by that misery. The unanswered demand of Job that the Almighty state his case was a reminder of the refutation always shouted by life itself at any neat orthodoxy.

Or—the style and content are such that it is hard to decide —the original author may be responsible for the speech of God in which Job's demand is answered. Whichever be the case, the answer of God is worthy of the question posed by the dialogue. It does not, like the speeches of the friends and the formulas of orthodoxy, present an answer to the problem of Job in which the reality of suffering and fear and human frustration is magically wiped out. It answers Job's question by asking him whether his human mind can comprehend the power and wisdom that lie behind the order of the universe, behind the allotting of boundaries to the sea, the division between light and darkness, behind the mysteries of life and procreation, behind all the wonder of the natural world (Job 38:1—42:6).

The point being made is that man is man and not God, and that the mind of man is not capable of containing the answers to all of the questions posed by life. True wisdom does not lie either in seeking an answer or in believing that one possesses an answer. True wisdom lies in accepting human creatureliness and in recognizing the majesty of God. True wisdom is the wisdom of Job, who lays his hand on his mouth and ceases to speak, who repents in dust and ashes at his presumptuousness in seeking an answer.

It is not really Job who is being rebuked in the speech of God. It is the three friends and the orthodoxy represented by them. It is in the speech of God which is the climax of the book in its finished form that the explicit theological point of the wisdom movement in post-exilic Israel is made, even though wisdom had already begun to be absorbed by orthodoxy. That point is that no doctrine of God's sovereignty over history which fails to take account of the realities of human existence really does justice to the facts of the case. Not only is such a doctrine inadequate, it is blasphemous. The facts of human life and the mystery of creation proclaim this. In the author of the dialogues of the book of Job and in the author of the speech of God, a poet—or poets—had been found whose art was great enough to make those facts and that mystery speak eloquently. That art shines through, even though the insertion of the Elihu speeches (Job 32-37) and the prose conclusion to the book seek to bring the content more into line with the orthodox doctrine.

The author of Ecclesiastes wrote against the same background as did those responsible for the book of Job.[17] He too was out to show up the bankruptcy of the orthodox answers. That he specifically discounts the ability of wisdom to be of any help would seem to indicate that he wrote at a time when wisdom had been pretty thoroughly identified with orthodoxy. He is even more skeptical than the writers of Job. He is a cynic, albeit a gentle cynic.

The author of Ecclesiastes is an Israelite, and not for a minute does he doubt the existence or the power of God. He simply despairs of every human attempt to formulate principles about the way in which God governs his world. The attempts of human wisdom to make sense of the mystery of life fail. They arrive only at foolishness. Every human plan, every human idea, every human definition of a plan or pattern by which life should be lived is vain. Indeed vanity—the Hebrew word means nothingness, non-existence, foolishness, absurdity, unprofitableness—is the key word in Ecclesiastes. It sums up the philosophy of the author. Life, in spite of the pompous claims of the post-exilic priests and scribes and wise men, has no discernible meaning. It is repetitive, vain, foolish. It leads to the same death for wise and foolish, rich and poor, industrious and lazy. Man should simply take life as it comes, enjoy it as much as he can, and not seek to make something profound out of it.

Ecclesiastes is almost wholly negative in its outlook. It is thoroughly skeptical. Yet it, like Job, points to the givenness of a world and a life which cannot be contained in the formulas or dogmas of an orthodox system. It may do so negatively, but it bears witness to the prophetic insistence that man cannot control the course of things or himself presume to give it meaning. It is an expression of doubt, and doubt is closer to that faith to which the living God can speak than is an overly confident dogmatism or a shallowly grounded optimism.

The importance of the wisdom literature is indicated by the fact that it became the nucleus of the third section of the Hebrew Bible. In addition to the canon of the law and the canon of the prophets, the Old Testament—in the form in which it exists in the Jewish community—contains a final division designated simply as "the writings." This part of the canon contains those books which, for the most part, were written later on in Israel's history and were the last to be given scriptural status. Among the writings are found the late history of the Chronicler, the little story of Ruth, the Lamentations over the fall of Jerusalem wrongly ascribed by late tradition to Jeremiah, and the rabidly nationalistic book of Esther.[18]

The core of the writings is, however, the wisdom literature—Proverbs, Job and Ecclesiastes—and the poetry the wisdom movement collected and preserved—Psalms and the Song of Songs. Just as the J Document in which narrative was employed to bear witness to the sovereignty of the God who had revealed himself to Israel became the nucleus of the first section of the scriptures, and just as the books resulting from the careers of the great prophets who had continued that witness formed another such section, so the wisdom literature which, in its own way, was bearing witness to the majesty of God became the basis of the third and final section of the scriptures of Israel.

APOCALYPTIC

In the third part of the Hebrew Bible, the writings, there is one book that falls into a class by itself. This is the book of Daniel. In the order of the books in the English Bible—which reflects an attempt of the translators of the Old Testament into Greek to group the literature into various types of books—Daniel is included with the prophetic writings. But, though its outward form may be somewhat like that of those books, it is far removed from the prophetic movement in time as well as in content.

Daniel is the only Old Testament book belonging to a type of literature known as apocalyptic (the word means "revelational"). At the very end of the pre-Christian era and in New Testament times, apocalyptic flourished. The Revelation of St. John the Divine in the New Testament is an example of Christian apocalyptic.[19]

Like the J Document and the prophetic movement, apocalyptic was called forth by its historical environment. And, like J and the prophets, it was convinced of the sovereignty of Israel's God in history, and sought to bear witness to that sovereignty. There, however, the parallels between prophecy and apocalyptic end. Whereas prophecy couched its message in the form of terse oracles or dramatic actions in which the truth of an historical present was given expression, apocalyptic employed allegory and cryptic visions to make its point.

Whereas a prophet openly addressed himself to the issue presented by some historical situation, apocalyptic was written by men who coded their message in fanciful tales and visionary scenes (the true meaning of which was apparent only to the initiated) and attributed what they said to some ancient worthy. Whereas prophecy interpreted some historical present as the result of God's unfolding purpose, apocalyptic concentrated on the imminence of the end of history to which its own time was important only as the immediate prelude. Whereas prophecy had seen Israel's choice by God as no assurance of privilege but only a terrible responsibility, apocalyptic concentrated on the way in which the imminent end would bring vindication to Israel—at least to the faithful in Israel—as well as retribution to those who had scoffed at her and persecuted her.

Apocalyptic was nurtured by disillusionment and hardship and frustration. The whole post-exilic history of Israel from 540 B.C. until 150 B.C. was disappointing to those to whom the prophetic interpretation of the fall of the nation had brought a vision of a chastened and purified people of God. Neither the priestly vision of a holy worshipping community nor the ideal of a people whose observance of the law of God would be witness to his sovereignty came to pass. Outward conditions of subjection, first to Persia and then to Alexander the Great and his successors, as well as apathy and cynicism and poverty within the Jewish community itself, conspired against the fulfillment of God's purpose for Israel. History did not seem to confirm Israel's faith in a God whose people's faithfulness and good fortune were to be signs of his sovereignty.[20]

The despair resulting from the shattering of high hopes, as well as the prophetic insistence that no human institution could perfectly fulfill the purpose of God, led to the conviction that the fulfillment was not to come *in* history, but *beyond* history. It would only be at the end of time, when God would bring the old age to a conclusion and inaugurate a new age, that the presumptuous empires of this world and the faithless in Israel would be shown what the truth really was. In that new age God would reign openly, would judge those who had not acknowledged his sovereignty, would reward those who had.

This transmutation of the original prophetic hope from expectation of the restoration of Israel in this world to expectation of a totally new age took place very gradually. In many instances it is difficult to tell to which kind of expectation the later passages in the prophetic books are referring. A section such as Isaiah 24-27 or Zechariah 9-14 or a book such as Joel is, however, verging on the later kind of expectation.

It was not just in isolated passages or books that the newer kind of hope in the sovereignty of God found expression. This hope apparently became focused in a schematic idea of the course history had been and was taking. There had been an ideal age (variously identified with primeval paradise or the era of Moses or the time of David) the perfection of which had been ruined by Israel's rebellion and perversity. A time of judgment and chastening for Israel had, therefore, been necessary. That time would, however, draw to a close, and would be followed by a time in which the pagan nations—who had foolishly interpreted the punishment of Israel as a sign of the weakness of Israel's God—would learn the awful lesson of God's sovereignty in a terrible holocaust. Then would come the time in which the original ideal age would return, made even more wonderful by the perfection of all that had intervened in history. The hoped for new era, the messianic age, was variously described just as the ideal age of the past was variously described. There was no one form of the messianic hope.[21]

This scheme, consciously or unconsciously, exerted great influence upon the actual organization of the Hebrew Bible. The Pentateuch depicted the ideal age, and the books of the former prophets (Joshua through Kings) the age in which Israel had rebelled. Its three final phases were described in the prophetic books, and it was in those books that the scheme was most influential. Though it may at times be varied, the plan of the prophetic books is generally one in which pronouncements against Israel are followed by pronouncements against foreign nations and then by prophecies of the restoration of Israel. This organization reflects the scheme of which we have been speaking: the prophets had come to enunciate the meaning of the age in which Israel was being judged and punished; and that age would be followed by one in which the nations would be judged; and the final step would be the new age.[22]

This scheme was really the reduction to formula of the prophetic faith in God's purpose as that which imparted meaning to history. It was, nevertheless, a source of real comfort to many to whom post-exilic developments had brought disillusionment. The low estate to which the fortunes of Israel had fallen could be explained by the fact that the final terrors of the time of judgment and punishment were at hand. The nations might now be doing their worst, but they were, like Israel, in the control of God and the day of their punishment was at hand. The very terribleness of the present was a sign that the hoped for future was near.

For the Jews of Palestine the nadir of post-exilic despair was reached in the middle of the second century B.C. It was at that time Antiochus IV (Epiphanes), one of the Seleucid successors of Alexander the Great, seeking to bring Hellenistic culture and religion to all his territory, wooed many Jews into apostasy and then banned the Israelite religion altogether. Jews were forced to renounce their faith or be put to death. It was against this that the revolt of which Judas Maccabee was the hero took place, and it was out of this time of persecution and terror that the book of Daniel came.[23]

The book of Daniel consists of two parts. There are, first of all, a series of stories (chapters 1-6) in which the faithfulness of Daniel and his three young friends to "the God of heaven" is held up as an example to the Jews of the second century. The stories also make it clear that God richly rewards those who remain faithful to him through suffering and terror.

The second, and more characteristically apocalyptic, part of the book is found in chapters 7 through 12. In a series of visions, the course of history up until the time of writing is traced in cryptic and fantastic symbols, and the proclamation is made that the time of Israel's suffering and humiliation is rapidly drawing to a close. In "time, two times and half a time" (just three years and a half), the nations will meet their nemesis, and the new age in which the "saints of the most high" will be exalted will begin.

Apocalyptic was, thus, a reaffirmation of the conviction of the J Document and the prophets that history had a meaning, that it was moving to the accomplishment of the purpose of the God who had revealed himself to Israel. Disillusioned by the failure of the vision of the priestly party to reach fulfillment, by the imperfect and troublous course met by those who sought to keep the law, by the way in which the wicked within and without Israel prospered in spite of the ethic of the wisdom movement—the apocalyptic writers looked to the day in which God himself would bring history to the goal toward which it had been moving.

Apocalyptic was not, however, prophetic in the deeper sense of the word. For it history as such was not the medium of revelation that it had been to J and the prophets. For apocalyptic, history was only the unrolling of a great scroll the content of which had already been worked out. History was not something vital in which the living God was ever doing new things to reveal the wonder of himself. It was simply the illustration of the validity of a scheme already worked out. Whereas J and the prophets had claimed knowledge of one in terms of *whom* history had meaning, apocalyptic claimed to be in possession of a secret *plan* according to which history was operating.

Furthermore, apocalyptic, like the wisdom movement, did not break out of the post-exilic orthodox system. It did not, like the prophetic movement in an earlier time, give the lie to current attempts to define precisely the ways of God. The point of the stories in the first six chapters of Daniel is that the keeping of the dietary and other provisions of the law is rewarded. Apocalyptically oriented communities, such as the one whose center has recently been discovered near the Dead Sea, had a fanatical devotion to the law—to the religion of the book. Indeed, their chief claim was that they were the part of Israel in which alone the law was being adequately observed.[24] Though apocalyptic sought to recover the ancient prophetic conviction of the sovereignty of the one true God in history, it was really much more an unsuccessful imitation of the *form* of prophecy than a recovery of its spirit.

The very variety of directions being taken by later strands of the Old Testament, and the frantically forced nature of their efforts, are indications that the Old Testament witness was pointing toward a fulfillment that had not yet come. The Old Testament faith, in its most profound statements, points beyond itself. The wisdom literature was a protest against premature certainties about the arrival of what lay beyond. Apocalyptic was a frantic statement, in frustrating times, of the certainty of the arrival of what lay beyond. But what lay beyond had yet to come.

CHAPTER SIX

The Main Line of the Biblical Witness

The journey we have made through the history of Israel—sometimes into dark and misty ancient places where historical reconstruction is extremely difficult—has not been motivated by a purely academic interest. The question we began with was, "How is God found?" That question, utterly serious and crucial for mankind, provided the framework for the whole discussion.

The question had, however, to be reframed in order for the Old Testament to be heard on its own terms. The claim of Israel was not that anyone had found God, but that God had made himself known—had revealed himself. It was as answer to the threefold question, "How, and where, and as whom, has God revealed himself?" that the Old Testament came into being during the course of eight centuries or more. The answer of the Old Testament was that God had revealed himself in and through the events of history; had revealed himself particularly in the course of history as it impinged upon the people Israel; had revealed himself as the One in terms of whom, and in terms of whose purpose, history's meaning was to be found.

The question could, for Israel, also be stated from the manward side. But stated from that side it could not be a "religious" question in the narrow sense of the word, not if it were to lead to the living God. For Israel the question which led to the place where God's revelation of himself could be seen would not be "How is God found?" or "What is the most helpful religion?" The relevant question was "What does history mean?" It was in terms of this latter question that the faith of Israel found expression in the narrative of the J Document and in the response of the canonical prophets to the events through which they lived. It was in terms of this latter question that Second Isaiah boldly asserted that the only God there was was the God who had made himself known to Israel. The others to whom the word was applied by men were only the products of human imagination and human craftsmanship: not because of their inferior religious value, but because they possessed no character, no purpose, in terms of which history made sense.

THE NECESSITY OF THE
HISTORICAL APPROACH

Any presentation of the Old Testament point of view has, therefore, to be an historical presentation. The answer given by the Old Testament to the question of the nature, character, and purpose of God is such that it cannot be contained in any series of concepts or propositions. The Old Testament is not bearing witness to certain truths *about* God, but to a history in which it believes God to have revealed him*self*. The appeal of the Old Testament is, in the final analysis, to that history. To take the book itself as the basis of the final appeal or to take any reduction of what the book is saying to a set of truths about God and his ways—even if those truths be couched in "biblical categories of thought"—as the basis of the final appeal, is to fail to take the Old Testament seriously on its own terms.

The appeal of the Old Testament is to history, and the history to which it appeals has to be taken seriously as history. The Old Testament itself raises the historical question, and to dismiss that question as an aberration of modern, unbelieving scholars is to take a position in which the Old Testament will never be understood for what it really is. It is on the basis of the point of view of the Old Testament itself that the search—made extremely difficult by the passage of centuries of time—must be undertaken for the true origins of the Sinai story, the real nature of the prophetic revolution, or the historicity of the claim that Moses instituted the ritual of the second temple. It is for this reason that, in the attempt of the foregoing chapters to get at the Old Testament point of view, the history to which the Old Testament appeals has been subjected to critical appraisal.[1]

The Old Testament not only appeals to past history as a basis for a knowledge of God. It points to present history as the only place in which those who are living in the present can know God in terms of the lordship over history through which he reveals himself. The clue, the definitive hints, are found in the events of the past as interpreted by a Moses. But the clue, the hints, are not ends in themselves. When memory, in which they are preserved, is combined by faith with the raw stuff of some present time, history takes on meaning. It is when the present through which men are living is seen as part of a whole over which and through which God is reigning, bringing his purpose to accomplishment, that the meaning of human life is dimly discerned.

It is in the prophets that this view of the historical present is most clearly taken. Yet, though it receives its most explicit statement in the prophets, it is a conviction of the presence and reign of God in the present that led to the writing of other parts of the Old Testament. The narrative of the J Document, the law of the Book of the Covenant in the E Document, Deuteronomy, the writings of the wise men, the visions of apocalyptic—all came into being in response to specific, historical situations. Furthermore, the combination of the various documents into the present Pentateuch and historical books, the organization of the prophetic books, the formation of the canon as a whole—these resulted from particular times in which the sovereignty of the God who had revealed himself in the past was being appealed to as that in which some present found its meaning.

All this provides a further justification for critical historical study of the Old Testament. The attempt to get at the times that brought forth the various writings of the Old Testament is not simply the result of a professional interest in the origins of things on the part of modern, faithless historians. Its justification—indeed, its real motive—lies in the point of view of the Old Testament itself. It is not some concept or some statement of truth—even itself as a statement of truth—to which the Old Testament appeals in the witness it bears to God. The appeal is to history, for it is as Lord of history that God has made himself known. It is not, therefore, just the words of the book—or the words of one of its component parts—that matter. It is when the book is read in terms of the history that produced a conviction of the sovereignty of God that it is indeed read from its own point of view.

The faith of the Old Testament is, then, an historical faith. It is inextricably bound up with history both in the appeal it makes to a particular series of events as the place where God has revealed himself to men and because particular configurations of events drove certain men to confess their faith in literary forms. Both in terms of the foundations upon which it rests its case and in terms of what caused that case to be stated, the Old Testament is a book for which history is crucially important. To say anything about the character of God or about the meaning of life, reference has, for the Old Testament, to be made to a particular history.

Furthermore, the lesson to be learned from that particular history is not abstracted or divorced from later history. What is to be learned about the character of God and the meaning of life is no negation of what is happening in any moment of history—though what is happening may be destructive of cherished institutions and ways of thought. The characteristic thing about the God who *is* God is that he is sovereign in history, that he is working out his purpose in history. And the meaning of life is to be found in terms of the history in which man's lot is cast; in terms of the past that has led to the place where man stands and of the future toward which his present is moving; in terms of the purpose of God which in all things and through all things and in spite of all things is moving onward to its accomplishment.

What that accomplishment is to be, what it is specifically to involve, cannot be predicted. No details, no plan, of the end toward which things are moving can be laid out. But the *one* whose purpose will prevail can be known. He has revealed him*self*. On the basis of the clues he has given in past events, something can be said of the meaning of any present to which history has led; something can be said of the shape the whole of history is assuming; the final outcome of things can be anticipated with certainty and with hopefulness. Because God reigns, the story up to the point at which its teller lives can be told as more than a chaotic succession of unrelated happenings. Because God reigns something significant can be said about the present and its outcome. And only on the basis of the story and the significance of the present and its outcome can anything significant be said about the God who reigns.

THE MAIN LINE

It is clear that two of the strands of the Old Testament are formative in the statement of this point of view. The J Document and the prophetic literature are the places where the presence of God in the course of history is most clearly discerned. They are the literary products of circles in which the

distinctively Hebraic interpretation of life was mo
pressed. They came out of times in which the actio.
brought forth expressions of that interpretation.

The way in which the J Document undertakes to explain the meaning of the Davidic kingdom in terms of the history that created it makes J the strand of the Old Testament which is not only creative of the faith of Israel but of the idea of history so integral to western civilization. J's principle of interpretation, by which all the various elements of history can be tied together, makes the Hebrews and their faith the source of the kind of interest in world history and its meaning which has been characteristic of post-medieval western thought. The way in which the story is told up to the point of the writing of the J Document and then left open-ended without imposition of any abstract dogma about its outcome makes the J writer an historian—not just the purveyor of a religion. And it makes the God of whom J is speaking more than one of the gods.

The view of history and the faith in God that had found expression in the J Document in terms of past history was applied to present history by the prophetic movement during the period in which the course of world events was spelling the doom of Israel as a nation. Recent scholarship has made it clear that the prophets were not innovators in the sense that they expounded an entirely new view of God and of man's life under God. They were dependent upon the view of God and his ways in history that had found expression in the J Document at least one, and probably two, centuries before Amos, the first of the canonical prophets, appeared. The contribution of the prophets lies in their application to present history of the point of view enunciated in the J Document. On the basis of their knowledge of God in terms of past events, the prophets could declare that the very events by which Israel was being brought to destruction were the work of the one who had chosen Israel to witness to his sovereignty.

The prophetic view of history and of God as the Lord of his-

..ory finds its most organized expression in Second Isaiah. There, probably for the first time explicitly, the conviction of the exclusive right of Israel's God to be designated as God is proclaimed. The reason for Hebraic monotheism is that only in terms of the unfolding purpose of Israel's God does the history in which man lives find any meaning, make any sense. Probably the result of years of prophetic activity and thought following the rise of Persia, Second Isaiah is the most organized, the most polished, the most definitely conceived and executed of the prophetic writings. In form as well as content it is an inspired and ingenious statement of the prophetic position. In it the ecstasy of the prophet, the art of the poet, a profound grasp of the distinctively Israelite point of view are combined.

Furthermore, Second Isaiah seems to be consciously dependent upon the J Document. Certainly it lays hold upon the thought and outlook of the J Document in a way that no other writing of the Old Testament does. It interprets that thought and outlook clearly and faithfully in terms of a new age of history, an age in which Israel has been made by history into something different from what she was in the time of the J writers. Like the J Document, Second Isaiah is a well-thought-out and carefully composed statement of the faith that goes back through prior history to the exodus and to the inspired insight of Moses into the meaning of the exodus. In terms of that faith alone, Second Isaiah asserts, does all history before and after the exodus make sense.

Thus a definite line runs from the J Document to the prophets, particularly to Second Isaiah. That line is the main line of biblical faith. It sees history as the area in which the God who really is God is working out his purpose. It assumes that that God is known only in terms of that historical purpose as he inspires men to see it. For it history has to unfold and the story recounted for God to be known. For it the whole truth about God and his purpose can be contained in no concept, no system, no statement. The whole truth about God and his purpose, though history has begun to reveal it, cannot be known until history is complete.

CRYSTALLIZATIONS

The main line runs from the J Document to the prophetic movement with its culmination in Second Isaiah. But the Old Testament does not consist only of the J Document and Second Isaiah. The whole of the biblical witness is not borne by them. Other strands of witness are present, strands that may not be as formative as J and the prophets but which preserved the witness when it was threatened by forces within or without the Israelite community.

The E Document and Deuteronomy, the literature going back to the old covenant-confederation of tribes in the north, is such a strand. It began to take literary form in opposition to the policies of the house of Omri in the ninth century. This strand of witness points to the same events as J. It finds the clue to history and to the meaning of Israel in history—in Moses and the exodus. But it also crystallizes the significance of those events into a concept of Israel as the community in which faith is confessed and the covenant law is practiced in its purity. The appeal is wholly to the past. Really, for this strand of the tradition, subsequent history was not the place where the purpose of God continued to unfold. It was simply the setting in which Israel was either obedient or disobedient to the law already given. Neither history itself nor the actors in it were in and of themselves important. In this strand of the tradition the faith enunciated by the J Document in terms of history was put into concepts. Because it had been crystallized into one set of terms, it could not take account of new things presented by history, and the prophets—particularly Amos— had to challenge it.

The Priestly Code also bore witness to the faith of Israel. It came into being as a result of the prophetic interpretation of the events that brought Israel to her national downfall. Indeed, it represented an honest and serious attempt to deal with the question of what Israel was to be when history had brought a revolutionary change in the manner of her existence. But the concept of Israel as a holy community, carrying on the appointed worship of the one true God, week by week, month by month, and year by year, was also a crystallization. Again, the terms in which the lessons of history had been expressed made any further history irrelevant. Whatever might be the course of world events, Israel was to worship God in the appointed way—to keep the prescribed ritual law. Again, history was only the backdrop against which Israel fulfilled her appointed task. All in it that was significant had happened when the second temple was built and its ritual begun. And when the concepts of the law-observing community and of the cult-performing community were combined in the compromise that produced the Pentateuch, this tendency was carried even further.

It was as a protest against the post-exilic crystallization of faith that the ancient wisdom of the wise men was made the basis of a theological position. In a time when the official formulations had left no real room for the recognition of truths about God and his ways outside the formulations themselves, the mystery of nature and the wonder of the wisdom by which it was ordered could become the basis of reverence and holy fear.

Yet, though its insistence on the majesty of God made it the bearer of the prophetic spirit in a time when the more accustomed expressions of that spirit had become crystallized, the point of view of the wisdom literature was fundamentally different from that of the J Document and the prophetic movement. When God is spoken of primarily in terms of nature and of the laws by which nature is regulated, and when the human problem is defined primarily in terms of the finitude that makes existence in nature so uncertain, history has been removed from the role it played in J and the prophets. It has become merely the setting of a human drama which is essentially the same whatever age may be its setting. History has become a static thing in which the purpose of the living God could not possibly be at work.

The wisdom literature might provide a magnificent protest. It might remind orthodoxy that no doctrine of God—even as Lord of history—in which room was not left for every reality of human existence could do justice to the facts. It might, in the tradition of J and the prophets, show up the inability of any statement or position to contain the whole truth. Yet the wisdom literature, because of the terms in which it thought and spoke, could never become a positive servant of that point of view by which the main line of the biblical witness is characterized. Especially was this so when wisdom had been absorbed into the very orthodoxy against which it had protested.

Finally, in the centuries in which the era of the Old Testament was drawing to a close, apocalyptic arose as an attempt to state anew the prophetic conviction of the lordship of Israel's God over history. It is such a conviction that lies behind the sometimes violent and sometimes fantastic fanaticism of apocalyptic literature. Yet the assurance with which that literature speaks of the imminent denouement of the course of history is quite different from the spirit of J and the prophets. It is assurance based on a preconceived definition of the plan underlying history and not on the kind of faith in *one* who reigns in the course of events—the faith that is characteristic of the main line of the biblical witness. Apocalyptic is really a crystallization of the prophetic faith into a rather hardened form, both thought and mode of expression being very stylized.

Thus, though there is a unity in the Old Testament in its witness to the same God, there is a diversity of emphasis, of theological perspective, of literary form. There is a unity in the appeal made—even indirectly in the wisdom literature—

to the formative events of Israel's history as the basis of a knowledge of God not only for Israel but for all peoples. There is a diversity, however, in the way in which differing historical ages and situations resulted in witness being borne to the formative events and to the work of God in them in various ways and terms.

THE CONTINUANCE OF THE MAIN LINE: THE NEW TESTAMENT

It is their awareness both of the significance of the original formative events and of the importance of every subsequent moment in history which make the J Document and the prophetic literature the two most influential points on the line of Old Testament history. The crystallizations of the faith of J and the prophets tended to identify witness to Israel's God with one particular age or emphasis or concept or expression of that witness. Consequently they were unable to account for developments in some later historical situation except as aids or obstacles to the particular position they had espoused. They were unable, to use a recurrent word in Second Isaiah, to account for "new things." They were always confounded by the "new thing" being done by God in some new event. In their certainty that they had been vouchsafed a revelation of God and of the truth about God, they tended to forget that the God of Israel was the living God and that the whole truth about him could not be told until the whole story in which he was involved—history—had reached its conclusion.

The history of Israel came, therefore, to be more and more the story of tragic disappointment and frustration. The meaning of her existence was to be found in "the things that are revealed." To that faith J and the prophets had borne witness. To that faith the various other strands of the Old Testament had also borne witness. But the openness of J and the prophets to what the further unfolding of history might bring was missing from the other strands of witness, from the strands that followed J and the prophets. It was as if the confidence that "the things that are revealed belong to us and to our children forever" was always seeking to find definitive embodiment in a theological position or an organization of life or a conception of Israel, only to be frustrated by the inescapable reservation that "the secret things belong to the Lord our God." To take seriously the heritage of Israel was to seek to establish a structure, a position, in which Israel could fulfill her vocation. But the movement of history seemed always to give the lie to any claim that that had been done.

This frustration accounts for the proliferation of sects and points of view in Judaism in the years immediately preceding the Christian era. The completion demanded by the faith of the J Document and the prophets had not been found in any of the crystallizations. There were, therefore, many attempts to find that completion. The Pharisees, the Sadducees, the community at Qumran that left the Dead Sea Scrolls, the movement begun by John the Baptist, the rabid nationalism of the zealots, the "philosophical" Judaism of a Philo—all were attempts to provide that completion to which the historical faith of J and the prophets had pointed. The fact that only one Jewish sect, rabbinic Judaism as it came out of the development of which the Pharisees were a part, survived tends to obscure for modern readers the complexity by which Judaism was characterized in the first Christian century.[2] Rabbinic Judaism—in which fulfillment of the ancient faith is found in the Talmudic interpretation of the law—has its roots in the Old Testament witness. But, like Christianity, it is a completion of that witness and is not to be thought of simply as the religion of the Old Testament.

If rabbinic Judaism is a completion of Old Testament faith not to be identified with the Old Testament, Christianity is also such a completion not to be separated from the Old Testament. Indeed, the New Testament would define Christianity simply as the fulfillment of the law and the prophets. The generation of the Church by which the New Testament was produced would never have dreamed of defining Christianity apart from the Old Testament. What man himself could not accomplish—what none of the crystallizations of the Old Testament faith had accomplished—God had accomplished in the life and death and resurrection of Jesus Christ and in the gathering of the community in which Christ is preached. That is the proclamation of the New Testament.[3]

In the spirit of the J Document and the prophets, the New Testament is not laying out a plan or framing a concept. It is pointing to a history—to the whole history of Israel—and maintaining that the latest development in that history is the work of the God who is history's Lord. Though what began in Galilee and moved to Jerusalem and is now moving out into the Mediterranean world does not fit into any of the preconceived notions of what the outcome of God's purpose will be, it is recognizable as the work of the God who acted in the exodus and in the events of the prophetic age. That is the New Testament proclamation. Like the kingdom of David which transformed Israel from a covenant-federation into something new that, at the same time, found its meaning in the old faith, and like the rise of the world empires that transformed Israel from a nation into a community of faith, this latest "new thing" is part of the purpose of God. That is the message of the New Testament, and it is in the tradition of the J Document and the prophetic movement. The New Testament is the third formative point on the main line of biblical witness. It is only as such that it can be understood in its context and on its own terms.[4]

Like the Old Testament, then, the New Testament is not a merely "religious" document. For the writers of the New Testament, Jesus is not a merely "religious" figure, and the Christian Church is not a merely "religious" community. For the writers of the New Testament, Jesus Christ is both the fullest revelation of the character of God and his purpose, and the culmination of that purpose. And the Christian Church is the community through which that—the truth about history—is to be proclaimed. The significance, therefore, of Jesus Christ and the events consequent upon his coming lies in the character of history itself. The meaning of time itself is revealed in Jesus and in what his coming means.[5]

It is here that the real significance of the many New Testament references to the prophets lies—not in the specific details of the prophetic passages themselves. Through its many citations of the prophets, the New Testament is relating its message to the witness of the prophets. It is claiming that its witness is part of that main line of witness that holds the Old Testament together. It is claiming to have discerned the Lord of history at work. It is claiming that Jesus Christ and the Church are related to the purpose which gives history its meaning and that, like the prophetic movement, they are the work of God to define that purpose.

So it is that the significance of Jesus Christ and what was accomplished in him is consciously related—possibly by Jesus himself—to the climax of the ancient prophetic witness in the Servant Songs of Isaiah 40-55, and that Isaiah 53 can be used to describe the significance of what happened on Good Friday. As Second Isaiah seems consciously to be related to the J Document, so the climactic passages of Second Isaiah seem consciously to be related to Christ. Though the servant concept was dropped fairly early as the chief interpretation of the work of Jesus, owing both to its ambiguous significance in Judaism and its lack of meaning to Gentiles, the real importance of its use lies in the way in which it is a means of relating Christianity to the prophetic movement.[6] Christ and the Christian movement are not, the New Testament says, just a "religious" phenomenon like the various sects of Judaism or the cults of the Hellenistic world with their various doctrines and techniques of spiritual discipline. They are part of that main line of witness to the purpose of God in history of which the J Document and the prophetic movement were parts.

The real origins of the Christian doctrine of the Holy Spirit are to be found in the same conviction. In the Old Testament the spirit of God was thought of in various ways. But the spirit came to be thought of chiefly as the source of prophetic inspiration. Since the real meaning of prophecy, from Amos on, lay in its function as a means through which God revealed to men the meaning of history, the spirit was associated with such revelation. The prophets—those upon whom the spirit came— were those through whom God revealed the truth about any given historical present:

> Surely the Lord God does nothing, without revealing his secret to his servants the prophets. (Amos 3:7)

Now the history whose meaning was revealed to the prophets was, by implication in the J Document and explicitly in later prophetic writings, moving toward a culmination in which the purpose of God would be seen in its fullness. When history would have reached that culmination, what had formerly been seen only by certain chosen servants would be seen by all. It is longing for this culmination that prompted the cry put into Moses' mouth in Numbers 11:29: "Would that all the Lord's people were prophets, that the Lord would put his spirit upon them!" The same conception of a culmination of history in which history's purpose would be seen as clearly by all as it had by the prophets lies behind the late prophecy of Joel:

> And it shall come to pass afterward that I will pour out my spirit upon all flesh, and your sons and daughters shall prophesy . . . (Joel 2:28)

When, therefore, the New Testament describes the experience that came to the earliest Christians as a result of the life and death and resurrection of Jesus Christ as a pouring out of the spirit of God, it is not defining Christianity as some mystical phenomenon or as the source of some mysterious, narrowly religious, spiritual power. It is connecting Christianity with that main line of biblical witness that began with the J Document and had primarily to do with the meaning of history. It is maintaining that in Jesus Christ the purpose of the Lord of history had reached a point of fulfillment from which the meaning of history could be seen. The Christian is more than just a devotee of another religion. He is, by faith in Christ, the recipient of a revelation of the meaning of the history of which he is a part.

> For he has made known to us in all wisdom and insight the mystery of his will, according to his purpose which he set forth in Christ as a plan for the fulness of time . . . (Ephesians 1:9,10)

It is in terms of this conviction that the early Christian expectation of the imminent end of history can be explained. Through Christ the Christians had been admitted to that vantage point of faith from which the purpose of God could be seen in its wholeness. They had been brought into a relationship with God in which the spirit was poured out upon all of them and in which all of them could "prophesy"—could bear witness to the true meaning of all things. History had for them, therefore, arrived at the point toward which it had been moving from the very beginning. This meant, given the prevalence of apocalyptic in the world of the early Christians, that the end must be at hand. Through their use of apocalyptic terminology—and Jesus himself used that terminology—the early Christians were asserting that what God had done in Christ had real bearing, decisive bearing, on the outcome of history itself.

What, then, was really being expressed by Jesus and the early Christians was not just the apocalyptic expectation in a new and Christian form. That expectation provided the only terms in which the conviction that the God of Israel, the Lord of history, had acted once more in a decisive manner could be expressed. The fact, therefore, that the end did not come immediately is not a proof of error on the part of the early Christians. It is evidence of the inadequacy of the thought forms of their time to contain what God had done in Christ. It is evidence that the essential Christian proclamation has to do with something that defies every attempt of human language or thought to define it. That with which the Christian proclamation has to do, like the exodus and the destruction of Israel in the past, was an act of God that confounded all attempts to classify it in terms of what man already knew. That to which Christians bear witness, the life and death and resurrection of Jesus Christ, gives meaning to the history that led up to it and to the history that followed it. The light shed by Jesus Christ on the meaning of history is what makes it clear that he is God's word to man. To use the terms of Second Isaiah, God had been at work in the coming of Jesus Christ because Christ was the clue to the significance both of the former things and of the latter things.

That was the essential Christian proclamation: that Jesus Christ was the revelation of the real meaning of history; that his life and death revealed the really significant issues for man in history; that his resurrection was the revelation of whose power was sovereign in history. That proclamation could move out of the cultural and intellectual area in which it first found expression westward to Greece and Rome and Europe and America and Asia, not just bringing another religion but shedding light on the meaning of history wherever and whenever men live. Indeed, so connected was that proclamation with history that it is in terms of what it has to say that the time in which history takes place has come to be identified.

Who Christ really is—and who the God who acted in Christ really is—is proclaimed in the way in which the pharaohs of Egypt, the philosophers of Greece, the emperors of China, and the Incas of Peru are all dated in relation to Christ and to the act of God in him. It is in terms of Christ and of the act of

God in him that B.C. and A.D. can be the means by which the various ways in which man has dated things—the regnal years of the Babylonian kings or the years of the Jewish calendar or the Muslim reckoning from the hegira—are related to one another. The way in which this is used by even the most unreligious and unbelieving historians is symbolic of what the God to whom the Bible bears witness—the God who acted in Christ—really is. He is neither the chief figure of a "religion" nor a divinity offering men some imaginary escape from the history in which their lot is cast. He is the Lord of that history, and therefore that history is moving toward the accomplishment of his purpose. The proclamation that history is moving to the accomplishment of *his* purpose is good news because of what he has revealed himself to be in the history of Israel and in the life and death and resurrection of Jesus Christ.

How is God found? For the main line of the biblical witness —for the J Document and the prophets and the New Testament—he is found only where he has revealed himself. He is found in the movement of history, for it is Lord of history that he has revealed himself to be. He is not, then, found in any "religious" escape from history—some approach that denies the significance of what man really is. God is known as man looks back in faith to those events in which God has revealed himself, to the course of history in which his purpose has been at work. God is known, not in the crystallized definitions into which man has put what he saw in those past events, but as man looks from those events to the present and future for the further unfolding of the purpose of God. God is known in the watchful and obedient and expectant faith that sees ongoing history as the place where he reigns. He is known in the working and the waiting in which those who trust in him confess their faith that the history in which they live is his.

The vocation of the Church—the community in which the biblical witness is preserved—and the vocation of the Church's members is not, therefore, a religious vocation in any restricted sense of the word. Like the vocation of ancient Israel, it is a vocation to bear a witness in which the world sees and hears a proclamation of who it is who is really God. That vocation involves preaching and worshipping and working and living as if history—not just the Church or individual men, but history —were God's. It means that the significance of history is found only in the purpose of the God who revealed himself in Israel and in Christ. It means that the real reason that time goes on —in this age of the New Israel—is that the gospel of Christ may be proclaimed. The claim of that gospel—and of the total biblical witness of which it is the climax—is that it provides the clue in terms of which life makes sense.

Author's Notes

Chapter One
THE WITNESS OF THE NARRATIVE

1 W. F. Albright, in *Interpreter's Bible,* v. 1, pp. 233-271; John Bright, *A History of Israel,* pp. 17-59.
2 *Ibid.* Cf. also, W. F. Albright, *Archeology of Palestine.*
3 G. E. Wright, *The Old Testament Against Its Environment.*
4 Genesis 29:31—30:24; 35:23-27; 46:8-25.
5 Martin Noth, *The History of Israel,* pp. 53-137; Bright, *History,* pp. 128-160.
6 The stories in Judges celebrate these ancient leaders. Cf. Judges 5; 6—8; 11—12.
7 Cf. the passages in note 4 above. In the lists the northern tribes of Issachar, Zebulun, Gad, and Asher are traced to Leah and Zilpah. This prevents the fitting of things into a neat pattern, but it is also true that these four are the most nebulous of the tribes and that a certain arbitrariness always entered into the rounding out of the lists into twelve tribes.
8 Noth, *History,* pp. 55-58; N. K. Gottwald, *A Light to the Nations,* pp. 160-165.
9 The location of Mt. Sinai near the southern tip of the Sinai Peninsula is documented no earlier than the sixth century A.D. Noth, *History,* pp. 127-131.
10 Against the majority opinion the present writer would hold that the exodus tradition (with which Moses' historical role was connected) originated with the southern tribes. T. J. Meek, *Hebrew Origins,* pp. 29-48; C. A. Simpson, *Revelation and Response in the Old Testament,* pp. 23-44. H. H. Rowley, *From Joseph to Joshua,* surveys the problem, and takes a different view.

11 Cf. the references in note 5 above. The view set forth here is closer to Noth than to Bright.
12 Judges 9.
13 I Samuel 13:19-22.
14 Psalm 78:60; Jeremiah 7:14; 26:6,9; I Samuel 4.
15 The story, in I Samuel 11, of Saul's first appearance as a leader is very much like the stories of the Judges.
16 Bright, *History,* pp. 163-174; Noth, *History,* 164-178.
17 Though part of the "late source," I Samuel 13:7b-15a and 15:1-35 reflect this.
18 I Samuel 17—31.
19 II Samuel 1 and 2.
20 II Samuel 3:1—5:5.
21 Genesis 14:17 ff. is an attempt to relate the pre-Davidic tradition of Jerusalem to Israel's own ancient past in the person of Abraham. Cf. also Joshua 10:1-5 and Psalm 110. On the theology and cult of Jerusalem cf. Aubrey Johnson, *Sacral Kingship in Ancient Israel.*
22 II Samuel 23:8-13.
23 The conquests of David are summarized in II Samuel 8. On David's reign cf. Bright, *History,* pp. 174-190; Noth, *History,* pp. 178-202, 215-223.
24 The splendor of Solomon's court is reflected in I Kings 1—11; cf. Bright, *History,* pp. 190-208; Noth, *History,* 203-223.
25 Here, it should be emphasized, reference is to the earliest narratives *to be written*—not to those appearing earliest in the present *order* of the Old Testament.
26 This narrative is found, for the most part, in I Samuel 4:1—7:1; 9:1—10:16; 10:26—11:15; 13:1—14:52; 16:14-23; 17 (in part); 18:6-16,20-29; 19:11-17; 21:1-9; 22:1—23:14; 25:2—27:12; 29:1—30:31; II Samuel 1—6; 8. It has been reconstructed in a readable form in R. H. Pfeiffer and W. G. Pollard, *The Hebrew Iliad.* On the critical problems cf. G. B. Caird in *Interpreter's Bible,* v. 2, pp. 855-860. The present writer is in substantial agreement with the analysis of Adolphe Lods, *Israel from its Beginnings to the Middle of the Eighth Century,* pp. 352-356.
27 Contrary to *The Hebrew Iliad,* a distinction should probably be made between the adulatory account of David in the "early source" through II Samuel 8 and the "court history" in II Samuel 9—20 and I Kings 1 and 2.

28 "J," or "the Yahwist," is so called because it refers to Israel's God as Yahweh or Jahveh (of which Jehovah is an erroneous rendering) from the very beginning. "E," or "the Elohist" (see the following chapter), on the other hand, holds that the proper name of God was first revealed to Moses, and uses the Hebrew word *Elohim* ("God") through Exodus 3:15.

29 For outlines of the contents of J as well as discussions of its contents cf. B. W. Anderson, *Understanding the Old Testament,* pp. 154-182; J. A. Bewer, *The Literature of the Old Testament,* pp. 60-73; Gottwald, *A Light to the Nations,* pp. 214-233. The present writer would hold that J carried the narrative through the conquest and the founding of the kingdom, incorporating the "early source" of the books of Samuel as its conclusion.

30 Though J's point of view was formed by the ancient Israelite faith as expressed in the ancient *credo* of Deuteronomy 26:5-9, his own creative accomplishment should be stressed. Cf. Gerhard von Rad, *Das formgeschichtliche Problem des Hexateuch,* pp. 46-62.

31 Scholars are not agreed on the question of how far J continued his narrative. Cf. note 29 above and N. H. Snaith in *The Old Testament and Modern Study* (ed. Rowley), pp. 84-105.

32 For a summary of various theories about strata within J itself as well as a "two edition" view of J in which the final writer would be definitely indebted to his predecessors, cf. C. A. Simpson in *Interpreter's Bible,* v. 1, pp. 190-196, and *Revelation and Response in the Old Testament,* pp. 94-110.

33 This would be true regardless of where J concluded his narrative.

Chapter Two

THE WITNESS OF THE LAW

1 Meek, *Hebrew Origins,* pp. 49-81.

2 Johannes Pedersen, *Israel: Its Life and Culture I-II,* pp. 279-310; *ibid. III-IV,* pp. 611-615.

3 G. E. Mendenhall, *Law and Covenant in Israel and the Ancient Near East.*

4 Gerhard von Rad, *Studies in Deuteronomy,* pp. 60-69; G. E. Wright in *Interpreter's Bible,* v. 2, p. 326.

5 On the various "themes" of tradition underlying the present Pentateuch, cf. Noth, *History,* pp. 109-137; von Rad, *Das formgeschichtliche Problem des Hexateuch.*

6 See note 10 to Chapter 1.

7 Von Rad, *Studies in Deuteronomy,* pp. 45-59.

8 Jerusalem was just such a city-kingdom, and a good deal of its pre-Israelite cultus and tradition was taken over by David.

9 It may be that the title "judge" has been applied to two types of leaders: charismatic leaders in battle and more regularly chosen administrators of the law. Bright, *History,* pp. 150-151; Noth, *History,* p. 101.

10 This is true of the deuteronomic editors of the books of Kings and even more true of the writers of Chronicles.

11 I Kings 15 and 16. Bright, *History,* pp. 210-219; Noth, *History,* pp. 224-236.

12 So designated in the annals of Tiglath Pileser III (744-727 B.C.)—in the century after Omri. J. B. Pritchard (ed.), *Ancient Near Eastern Texts,* p. 284.

13 Andre Parrot, *Samaria, The Capital of the Kingdom of Israel;* G. E. Wright, *Biblical Archeology,* pp. 151-156.

14 On the significance of the marriage, see Eric Voegelin, *Order and History,* I, 322-325.

15 Here, as in Chapter 1, a more positive view is taken of the Davidic achievement than that taken by others. Cf. Bright, *History,* pp. 203-208.

16 Cf. the Elijah stories, I Kings 17—19.

17 The stories of Elijah and Elisha occupy most of I Kings 17— II Kings 9. Cf. also II Kings 13:14 ff.

18 This is emphasized by Voegelin, *Order and History,* I, 325-334.

19 Edmond Jacob, *Theology of the Old Testament,* pp. 270-275; Gunnar Ostborn, *Tora in the Old Testament.*

20 Cf. in particular I Kings 18.

21 Cf. Chapter 1.

22 On E and its contents, cf. Anderson, *Understanding the Old Testament,* pp. 225-227; Bewer, *The Literature of the Old Testament,* pp. 74-86; Gottwald, *A Light to the Nations,* pp. 246-254.

23 The present writer would hold that E, like J, continues into the historical books and that the "late source" of the books of Samuel as well as a good deal of the material in the books of the Kings is connected with E. Cf. Snaith in *The Old Testa-*

ment and Modern Study (ed. Rowley), pp. 84-105, for a survey of opinions.

24 The intention here is not to argue for a specific date for E, which may very well have been written *after* the fall of the northern kingdom, but to point out that E's point of view finds its roots in the reaction in the north to the house of Omri.

25 The most characteristic passages from the "late source" in the books of Samuel are I Samuel 8, 12 and 15:1—16:13. Cf. *Interpreter's Bible,* v. 2, pp. 860-861.

26 Von Rad, *Studies in Deuteronomy* and in *Interpreter's Bible,* v. 2, pp. 320-326. On the connection of Deuteronomy and the Josian reform, the present writer would still incline toward the view of Gustav Hoelscher, "Das Buch der Koenige," in *Eucharistereon I,* pp. 206-213, although he would differ with Hoelscher on the date of Deuteronomy's origin.

27 On Deuteronomy, cf. *Understanding the Old Testament,* pp. 309-317; *A Light to the Nations,* pp. 334-346; *Interpreter's Bible,* v. 2, pp. 311-330.

Chapter Three

THE WITNESS OF THE PROPHETS

1 Daniel is, in fact, apocalyptic. See Chapter 5 below.

2 H. E. W. Fosbroke in *Interpreter's Bible,* v. 1, pp. 201-206; W. F. Albright, *From the Stone Age to Christianity,* pp. 301-305.

3 This is true of what the word could mean at one point, even though the ultimate etymological meaning of the word "prophet" is probably "one called (by God)." *From the Stone Age to Christianity,* p. 303.

4 A. C. Welch, *Kings and Prophets of Israel,* pp. 109-111.

5 Thus the present writer would insist that a sharper distinction has to be made between Amos and his successors and the earlier prophetic movement than that made by Albright, and that this distinction is of fundamental importance. Cf. *From the Stone Age to Christianity,* p. 306.

6 The order of the prophetic books in the Old Testament does not reflect the order in which the prophets whose names they bear appeared in history.

7 Bright, *History*, p. 251.
8 On the prophets and their times cf. E. W. Heaton, *The Old Testament Prophets;* T. H. Robinson, *Prophecy and the Prophets in Ancient Israel;* R. B. Y. Scott. *The Relevance of the Prophets.*
9 There would be debate about this. For surveys of scholarly opinion cf. H. H. Rowley, *The Servant of the Lord,* pp. 89-128, and Otto Eissfeldt in *The Old Testament and Modern Study* (ed. Rowley), pp. 134-145.
10 G. Henton Davies in *Studies in Old Testament Prophecy* (ed. Rowley), pp. 37-51.
11 Bright, *History,* pp. 251-319; Noth, *History,* pp. 253-288.
12 *Interpreter's Bible*, v. 1, pp. 207-211; J. H. Eaton, *Vetus Testamentum* IX, No. 2, pp. 138-157.
13 Bright, *History,* pp. 334-344; Noth, *History,* pp. 299-307.
14 Cf. references in the previous note.
15 James Muilenberg in *Interpreter's Bible,* v. 5, pp. 382-384.
16 *Ibid.,* p. 400.
17 This is not to say that monotheism was not implicit in Israel's faith from the beginning. It is, however, in Second Isaiah that Israelite monotheism finds its first completely explicit expression. G. E. Wright, *The Old Testament Against Its Environment,* pp. 30-41, treats this problem.
18 The Servant Songs are found in Isaiah 42:1-4; 49:1-6; 50:4-9; 52:13—53:12.

Chapter Four

THE WITNESS OF THE PRIESTLY SYNTHESIS

1 Bright, *History,* pp. 324-325; Noth, *History,* pp. 288-298.
2 Simpson in *Interpreter's Bible,* v. 1, pp. 197-198.
3 *Ibid.* The majority would tend to date the redaction of J and E before the exile. Cf. Anderson, *Understanding the Old Testament,* p. 383.
4 Those responsible for the present books of the Kings are usually referred to as the deuteronomic historians because their point of view is derived from Deuteronomy. Cf. Bewer, *The Literature of the Old Testament,* pp. 214-233. For the newer point of view in which Deuteronomy and the historical books are even more closely associated, cf. G. E. Wright, *The Book of the Acts of God,* pp. 99-130.

5 Admittedly, this is conjectural—but so is any reconstruction. Cf. *Interpreter's Bible,* v. 1, pp. 197-198.

6 Bright, *History,* pp. 325-331; Noth, *History,* pp. 294-298.

7 On the cultus and traditions of the Jerusalem temple, cf. W. F. Albright, *Archeology and the Religion of Israel,* pp. 142-155; Wright, *Biblical Archeology,* pp. 136-145.

8 Anderson, *Understanding the Old Testament,* pp. 381-382.

9 Bright, *History,* pp. 341-355; Noth, *History,* pp. 299-315.

10 Bright, *History,* pp. 356-386; Noth, *History,* pp. 315-335.

11 On Isaiah 56-66 cf. Muilenberg in *Interpreter's Bible,* v. 5, p. 414; on Malachi, R. C. Dentan in *Interpreter's Bible,* v. 6, pp. 1117-1120.

12 Note 5 above.

13 On the priestly code and its contents, cf. *Understanding the Old Testament,* pp. 383-393; *The Literature of the Old Testament,* pp. 259-279; Gottwald, *A Light to the Nations,* pp. 448-463.

14 *Interpreter's Bible,* v. 1, pp. 185-200; *Understanding the Old Testament,* pp. 379-383.

15 Cf. note 26 to Chapter 2 and *Interpreter's Bible,* v. 1, pp. 197-200.

16 W. O. E. Oesterley, *A History of Israel,* II, 419-423.

17 Bright, *History,* pp. 393-394; Noth, *History,* pp. 349-354.

18 W. A. L. Elmslie in *Interpreter's Bible,* v. 3, pp. 341-348; R. A. Bowman, *ibid.,* pp. 551-567.

19 The psalms are so vast a field of study in themselves that they have not been treated here. For a shorter and a longer study, each embodying the results of recent research, cf. S. L. Terrien, *The Psalms and Their Meaning for Today* and E. A. Leslie, *The Psalms.*

Chapter Five

LATER ATTEMPTS TO WITNESS

1 On the complicated question of the history behind the accounts of the restoration of Jerusalem in the books of Ezra and Nehemiah, cf. Bowman in *Interpreter's Bible,* v. 3, pp. 560-566; Bright, *History,* pp. 375-386; Noth, *History,* pp. 315-335.

2 Isaiah 13-23, Jeremiah 46-51, Ezekiel 25 32.

3 On Nahum, cf. C. L. Taylor, Jr., in *Interpreter's Bible,* v. 6, pp.

953-956; on Obadiah, J. A. Thompson, *ibid.*, pp. 857-859; on Esther, B. W. Anderson, *ibid.*, v. 3, pp. 823-832.
4 On Ruth, cf. L. P. Smith, *ibid.*, v. 2, pp. 829-831.
5 On Jonah, cf. J. D. Smart, *ibid.*, v. 6, pp. 871-874.
6 W. A. Irwin, *ibid.*, v. 1, pp. 212-219.
7 I Kings 12.
8 Ludwig Kohler, *Hebrew Man*, pp. 102-107; C. T. Fritsch in *Interpreter's Bible*, v. 4, pp. 771-772.
9 *Ibid.*, pp. 774-775.
10 On the theological significance of the wisdom literature, cf. J. C. Rylaarsdam, *Revelation in Jewish Wisdom Literature*; Wright, *The Book of the Acts of God*, pp. 177-190.
11 T. J. Meek in *Interpreter's Bible*, v. 5, pp. 91-98.
12 Terrien, *The Psalms and Their Meaning for Today*, pp. 239-264.
13 G. F. Moore, *Judaism*, I, 263-268.
14 R. H. Pfeiffer, *Introduction to the Old Testament*, pp. 619-620.
15 S. L. Terrien in *Interpreter's Bible*, v. 3, pp. 884-892.
16 For an outline of the book of Job, cf. *ibid.*, pp. 902-905.
17 O. S. Rankin, *ibid.*, v. 5, pp. 3-20.
18 On the history of the Old Testament canon, cf. Pfeiffer, *Introduction*, pp. 50-70.
19 H. H. Rowley, *The Relevance of Apocalyptic*.
20 Bright, *History*, pp. 387-412; Noth, *History*, pp. 335-399.
21 Joseph Klausner, *The Messianic Idea in Israel;* Sigmund Mowinckel, *He That Cometh*.
22 H. G. May in *Interpreter's Bible*, v. 6, p. 200.
23 Arthur Jeffrey, *ibid.*, pp. 341-354.
24 On the Dead Sea Scrolls and the community that produced them cf. Millar Burrows, *The Dead Sea Scrolls* and *More Light on the Dead Sea Scrolls*; Frank M. Cross, Jr., *The Ancient Library of Qumran*.

Chapter Six

THE MAIN LINE OF THE BIBLICAL WITNESS

1 For an important consideration of the theological significance of the historical method, cf. R. R. Niebuhr, *The Resurrection and Historical Reason*.
2 Wright, *The Book of the Acts of God,* pp. 191-196.

3 C. H. Dodd, *According to the Scriptures.*
4 The significance of the expansion of Christianity outside the bounds of Israel as part of the ongoing purpose of God in history is most explicitly discussed in the New Testament in Romans 9—11, a part of the epistle often neglected due to overly "religious" concentration on Romans 5—8. The profuse quotation of the Old Testament in Romans 9—11, and particularly of the prophets, is symbolic of the point being made in this paragraph.
5 Oscar Cullman, *Christ and Time.*
6 Oscar Cullman, *The Christology of the New Testament,* pp. 51-82; W. Zimmerli and J. Jeremias, *The Servant of God.* The negative conclusions of Morna Hooker, *Jesus and the Servant,* provide a necessary warning against excesses, but are not convincing.

Bibliography

Albright, W. F. *Archeology of Palestine*. Harmondsworth: Penguin Books, 1949.

——— *Archeology and the Religion of Israel*. Baltimore: The Johns Hopkins Press, 1953.

——— *From the Stone Age to Christianity* (Anchor Book). Garden City: Doubleday & Co., 1957.

Anderson, B. W. *Understanding the Old Testament*. Englewood Cliffs: Prentice-Hall, Inc., 1957.

Bewer, J. A. *The Literature of the Old Testament* (revised edition). New York: Columbia University Press, 1933.

Bright, John. *A History of Israel*. Philadelphia: The Westminster Press, 1959.

Burrows, Millar. *The Dead Sea Scrolls*. New York: The Viking Press, 1955.

——— *More Light on the Dead Sea Scrolls*. New York: The Viking Press, 1958.

Cross, F. M., Jr. *The Ancient Library of Qumran*. London: Duckworth & Co., 1958.

Cullman, Oscar. *Christ and Time* (trans. F. V. Filson). London: S. C. M. Press, 1951.

——— *The Christology of the New Testament* (trans. S. C. Guthrie & C. A. M. Hall). Philadelphia: The Westminster Press, 1959.

Dodd, C. H. *According to the Scriptures*. London: Nisbet & Co., 1952.

Eaton, J. H. "The Origin of the Book of Isaiah," *Vetus Testamentum* IX, No. 2. Leiden: E. J. Brill, 1959.

Gottwald, N. K. *A Light to the Nations: An Introduction to the Old Testament*. New York: Harper & Bros., 1959.

Heaton, E. W. *The Old Testament Prophets*. Harmondsworth: Penguin Books, 1958.

Hoelscher, Gustav. "Das Buch der Koenige" in *Eucharisterion I* (ed. Hans Schmidt). Goettingen: Vandenhoeck & Ruprecht, 1923.

Hooker, Morna. *Jesus and the Servant*. London: SPCK, 1959.

Interpreter's Bible. New York and Nashville: The Abingdon Press, 1952-1957.

Jacob, Edmond. *Theology of the Old Testament* (trans. A. W. Heathcote & P. J. Allcock). New York: Harper & Bros., 1958.

Johnson, Aubrey. *Sacral Kingship in Ancient Israel*. Cardiff; University of Wales Press, 1955.

Klausner, Joseph. *The Messianic Idea in Israel* (trans. W. F. Stinespring). New York: The Macmillan Co., 1955.

Köhler, Ludwig. *Hebrew Man* (trans. Peter R. Ackroyd). London: SCM Press, 1956.

Leslie, E. A. *The Psalms*. New York and Nashville: Abingdon-Cokesbury Press, 1949.

Lods, Adolphe. *Israel from its Beginnings to the Middle of the Eighth Century* (trans. S. H. Hooke). London: Routledge & Kegan Paul Ltd., 1932.

Meek, T. J. *Hebrew Origins* (revised edition). New York: Harper & Bros., 1950.

Mendenhall, G. E. *Law and Covenant in Israel and the Ancient Near East*. Pittsburgh: The Biblical Colloquium, 1955.

Moore, G. F. *Judaism*. Cambridge: Harvard University Press, 1927.

Mowinckel, Sigmund. *He That Cometh* (trans. G. W. Anderson). Oxford: Basil Blackwell, 1956.

Niebuhr, R. R. *The Resurrection and Historical Reason*. New York: Charles Scribner's Sons, 1957.

Noth, Martin. *The History of Israel* (trans. Stanley Godman). London: A. & C. Black, 1958.

Oesterley, W. O. E., and T. H. Robinson. *A History of Israel*. Oxford: The Clarendon Press, 1932.

Ostborn, Gunnar. *Tora in the Old Testament: A Semantic Study*. Lund: Hakan Ohlsson, 1945.

Parrot, Andre. *Samaria, the Capital of the Kingdom of Israel* (trans. S. H. Hooke). London: S.C.M. Press, 1958.

Pedersen, Johannes. *Israel: Its Life and Culture*. London: Oxford University Press, 1926 and 1940.

Pfeiffer, R. H. *Introduction to the Old Testament*. New York: Harper & Bros., 1941.

———— and W. G. Pollard. *The Hebrew Iliad*. New York: Harper & Bros., 1957.

Pritchard, J. B. (ed.). *Ancient Near Eastern Texts* (2nd edition). Princeton: Princeton University Press, 1955.

Rad, Gerhard von. *Das formgeschichtliche Problem des Hexateuch*. Stuttgart: W. Kohlhammer Verlag, 1938.

———— *Studies in Deuteronomy* (trans. David Stalker). London: S.C.M. Press, 1953.

Robinson, T. H. *Prophecy and the Prophets in Ancient Israel*. London: Duckworth & Co., 1923.

Rowley, H. H. *From Joseph to Joshua*. London: Oxford University Press, 1950.

———— (ed.). *The Old Testament and Modern Study*. Oxford: The Clarendon Press, 1951.

———— *The Relevance of Apocalyptic* (2nd edition). London: Lutterworth Press, 1947.

———— *The Servant of the Lord and Other Essays on the Old Testament*. London: Lutterworth Press, 1952.

———— (ed.). *Studies in Old Testament Prophecy*. Edinburgh: T. & T. Clark, 1950.

Rylaarsdam, J. C. *Revelation in Jewish Wisdom Literature*. Chicago: University of Chicago Press, 1946.

Scott, R. B. Y. *The Relevance of the Prophets*. New York: The Macmillan Co., 1944.

Simpson, C. A. *Revelation and Response in the Old Testament*. New York: Columbia University Press, 1947.

Terrien, Samuel. *The Psalms and Their Meaning for Today*. Indianapolis and New York: The Bobbs-Merrill Co., 1952.

Voegelin, Eric. *Order and History,* Vol. I: *Israel and Revelation*. Baton Rouge: Louisiana State University Press, 1956.

Welch, A. C. *Kings and Prophets of Israel*. London: Lutterworth Press, 1952.

Wright, G. E. *Biblical Archeology*. Philadelphia: The Westminster Press, 1957.

———— *The Old Testament Against Its Environment*. Chicago: Henry Regnery Co., 1950.

———— and R. H. Fuller. *The Book of the Acts of God*. Garden City: Doubleday & Co., 1957.

Index to Biblical Passages

General Index

Canaanites, 19
Christian proclamation, 154
Christianity, 149
Chronicle, court, 117, 119
Chronicler, 112, 123
Church, 150, 151; vocation of, 155
Circumcision, 99, 110; and covenant: *see* Covenant
Confederation, northern: 16, 20; attitude toward kingship, 48; covenant, 145; old, 22; premonarchial, 72
Confederations, tribal: unified, 24
Covenant, 17, 20, 41-47; book of the, 61, 65, 140; and circumcision, 107; cult of, 44; definition of, 41; -federation, 145, 150; Mosaic, 108; of Noah, 110; between Yahweh & Israel, 42; *see also* Priestly Code
Creation, 105
Cross, Frank M., 164
Cullman, Oscar, 165
Cyrus, 85, 87, 89, 101, 102

Damascus, 75
Daniel, book of, 113, 132-137; quasi-prophetic book of, 67
David, 15, 22-26, 28, 29, 53, 55, 69, 75, 93, 94, 98 116; covenant with, 95; great grandmother of, 117; at Hebron, 49; kingdom of, 93, 150
Davies, G. Henton, 162
Dead Sea Scrolls, 149
Deborah, 46, 47
Dentan, Robert C., 163
Deuteronomic code, 93
Deuteronomic *Credo,* 31
Deuteronomy, book of, 40, 43, 45, 63-64, 94, 95, 103, 109, 110, 111, 113, 115, 121, 126, 140, 145; and covenant-law tradition, 64; emphasis in, 65
Dietary laws, 99, 106

Dodd, C. H., 165

E Document, 45, 58-64, 93, 95, 103, 107-111, 113, 118, 121, 126, 140, 145; combination with J Document, 94; and decalogue, 61; and Deuteronomy, 65; emphasis in, 65; emphasis on law and covenant, 62; and exodus, 60-61; laws of, 110; in Numbers, 61; point of view, 59; religious interest of, 60; and traditions of sons of Israel, 62
Ecclesiastes, book of, 127, 130-131
Ecclesiasticus (wisdom of Jesus ben Sirach), 126
Ecstasy 69, 77; of the prophet, 144
Edomites, 28, 75, 116
Egypt, 20, 60, 75, 76, 85; pharaohs of, 154
Eissfeldt, Otto, 162
Elam, ruler of, 85
Elath, 25
El berith, 44
Elihu, speeches of, 130
Elijah, 45, 54-58, 63, 71-72, 127
Eliphaz, 128
Elisha, 54, 56-58, 63, 71-72
Elmslie, W. A. L., 163
Elohist, *see* E document
Esdraelon, 26
Esther, book of, 116, 131
Exclusivism, post-exilic, 115, 117
Exilic Community, 95-101
Exodus, 32-33, 145; book of, 40, 110
Ezekiel, 67, 77, 96, 100
Ezra, 102, 112, 115

Fertile Crescent, 17, 34, 75
Foreign wives, 115
Fosbroke, H. E. W., 161
Fritsch, C. T., 164

Gad, 157
Galilee, 150

Genesis, book of, 38, 105, 110, 112
Gerazim, Mount, 111
God, universal sovereignty of, 116
Good Friday, 151
Gottwald, N. K., 157, 159, 160, 163
Greece, 20, 154; philosophers of, 154. *See* also Hellenism.

Habakkuk, 77
Haggai, 102
Heaton, E. W., 162
Hebrew Bible, 132
Hebrews, 21; enslavement in Egypt, 34; point of view, 119, 120
Hebron, 17, 19, 33, 35; royal city, 23; tradition of, 17
Hellenism: cults, 151; culture and religion, 135; point of view, 119
Hezekiah, 124
Historical approach, necessity for, 139-142
Historicism, 33
History, culmination of, 152; and New Testament, 153
Hittite: empire, 42; peoples, 19; treaties, 42
Hoelscher, Gustav, 161
Holiness Code, 100, 103
Holy Spirit, origins of Christian doctrine of, 152
Hooker, Morna, 165
Horeb, 45
Horites, 19
Hosea, 42, 76, 110
Hurrian, law of, 41

"Instruction of Amen-em-Opet," 124
Irwin, W. A., 164
Isaac, 34
Isaiah, 67, 76, 82, 96
Isaiah, Second, 88, 90, 92, 101, 121, 139, 144, 148, 151, 154; prophetic view of history, 43

Israel, 27, 79; assembly of, 49; as chosen people, 115; as the exilic party, 103; God's purpose for, 80; history of, 148; as the holy people, 100, 113; kings of, 69; law in, 41; origins of law in, 41; premonarchical, 15-20; prophetic condemnations of, 79; sons of, 16, 19, 21, 24, 31, 41, 44, 46-51, 55, 62, 68 75, 109, 119; vision of a new, 103
Israelite: community, 100; nationalism, 82; piety, 82; point of view, 144; three primary marks of, 99
Israelites, Palestinian, 104
Issachar, 157
Ittai, 25

J Document, 26, 29-39, 58, 59, 64, 75, 78, 79, 87, 88, 90, 91, 95, 104-106, 108-110, 113, 115, 117, 119-121, 125, 131, 132, 136, 139, 140, 142-144, 146, 150-153; combination with E Document, 94; creation story in, 106; in Numbers, 61; point of view, 59; view of history, 143
J writer, 30-39, 44, 50, 60, 118, 145, 148; and eschatology, 38; and history, 38; and the human problem, 36; and the monarchy, 35; philosophy of history, 33; theology of, 37
Jacob, 33, 34
Jacob, Edmond, 160
Jeffrey, Arthur, 164
Jehu, 55, 62, 72, 73
Jeremiah, 42, 67, 77, 82, 96, 131
Jeremias, J., 165
Jeroboam, 48, 51, 54, 69
Jerusalem, 23, 24, 28, 48, 50, 76, 97, 109, 150; ancient faith of, 98; centrality of, in historical books, 112; cult of, 25, 98, 99,

103, 104, 106, 115; destruction of, 77, 85; fall of, 92, 95; post-exilic temple at, 112; priests of, 97; rebuilding of destroyed temple, 99; sanctuary at, 101; siege of, 76; temple of, 92, 93, 98, 99, 111

Jesus Christ, 150, 151, 154; life, death, and resurrection, 150, 152, 154

Jewish calendar, 155

Jezebel, 53, 54

Job, book of, 127-131; and wisdom movement, 127; writers of, 130

Joel, book of, 134

John the Baptist, 149

John, Gospel of, 126

Johnson, Aubrey, 158

Jonah, book of, 117, 118

Joseph, house of, 19

Joshua, book of, 135

Josiah, King: reformation of, 63, 111

Judah, 27, 98; house of, 17, 19, 21, 31, 68, 75, 109; kings of, 69

Judaism, philosophical, 149; rabbinic, 149; sects of, 149, 151

Judas Maccabee, 135

Judges, book of, 19, 21, 47

Kadesh, 18

Kadish-barnea, 18, 35, 45

Kenite, 17, 19

King, 27, 97; recognition of, 49

Kingdom: covenant tradition under, 47-56; division of, 50

Kings, book of, 39, 95, 112, 118, 120, 123, 125, 135

Kingship, 20, 28, 46; sacral, 24

Klausner, Joseph, 164

Kohler, Ludwig, 164

Lamentations, book of, 96, 113, 131

Law: basis of, 41-47; canon of, 121; literary form of, 113; witness of, 40-66; see Torah, meaning of

Leah, 17, 157

Lemuel, 124

Leslie, E. A., 163

Levi, caste of, 45

Levites, 108

Leviticus, book of, 40, 98, 110

Lods, Adolphe, 158

Malachi, 103

Mashal, 119, 123, 127. See Proverb

May, H. G., 164

Medes, 76

Meek, T. J., 157, 159, 164

Megiddo, 26

Melchizedek, order of, 96

Mendenhall, G. E., 159

Mesopotamia, 17, 76

Micah, 76

Micaiah, 69, 70, 73; story of, 71, 77

Midianite, 17, 19

Moabites, 28, 75

Monarchy: Davidic, 78; as defection, 63; earlier accounts of, 26-29; and prophets (see Prophets); rise of, 20-26

Monotheism, Hebraic, 144

Moore, G. F., 164

Moses, 18, 32, 40, 45, 54, 56, 60, 61, 63-66, 80, 93, 100, 104, 107, 110, 144, 145, 152; and the second temple, 140

Mowinkel, Sigmund, 164

Muilenberg, James, 162, 163

Muslim, 155

Nabopolassar, 76

Nahum, 77, 116

Nathan, 69

Nationalism, growth of, 116

Nebuchadrezzar, 76; first invasion of, 95
Nehemiah, 102-104, 109, 112, 115, 116
New Testament, 148-56; proclamation of, 150
Niebuhr, R. R., 164
Nile, River, 75
Nineveh, 76, 116, 117
Noah, 106
Noth, Martin, 157, 158, 160, 163
Numbers, book of, 40, 110

Obadiah, 116
Oesterley, W. O. E., 163
Old Testament: critical historical study of, 141; earliest continuous narratives, 27; faith, 141, 149; as national epic, 26; final synthesis of, 109-114; law in, 40; narrative, 26; not primitive, 14; point of view, 139; religion of, 37; world, 14
Omri, 52-53, 55, 57, 59, 61, 63, 64, 66, 71, 72, 80, 93, 145; house of, 73
Omriads, 56, 62
Orthodoxy, 128, 147; closed, 121; post-exilic, 137
Ostborn, Gunnar, 160

Palestine, 20, 35; community of, 92-95; return to, 101
Palestinian party, 104, 109, 113, 121; book of, 110; theology of, 109
Parrot, Andre, 160
Passover feast, 18, 108
Pedersen, Johannes, 159
Pentateuch, 32, 35, 40, 63, 108, 109, 112, 113, 134, 141, 146; birth of, 110; ritual regulations of, 98
Persia, 85, 87, 89, 133, 144; em-

pire of, 111; rise of, 85, 92; rule of, 101
Persian Gulf, 75
Pfeiffer, R. H., 164
Pfeiffer, R. H. and W. G. Pollard, 158
Pharaoh, 18
Pharisees, 149
Philistines, 20, 75; expansion of, 47; resistance to, 21
Philo, 149
Post-exilic despair, 135
Priestly Code, 44, 59, 104-109, 112, 115, 121, 145; and covenant, 105; creation story in, 106; and law, 108; and Noah, 106; outline of, 105
Priestly party, 104, 110-113, 115; vision of, 109, 112
Priestly synthesis: witness of, 91-114
Priests, Levitical, 18; plans of in exilic community, 98
Pritchard, J. B., ed., 160
Prophecy, 67; continuation of, 81-85; early meaning of, 68; and spirit of God, 69
Prophetic: books, 83, 85, 116, 135; circles, 84; conviction, 89; faith, 116; literature, 67; movement, 85, 120, 132, 146; party, 55, 62, 72; revolution, 54, 95; spirit, 146
Prophetism, new element in, 72
Prophets, 67, 136, 150, 152; bands of, 68-70, 72; canon of the, 113, 121; canonical, 78, 81, 143; comforters to Israel, 83; court, 69, 70; and destruction of Jerusalem, 82; message of the pre-exilic, 77-90; and monarchy, 69; pro-Davidic, 69; in recent scholarship, 143; and royal court, 69; sons of the, 72; witness of, 67-90; words of, 117

Proverbs, book of, 120, 123, 124, 131
"Proverbs of Solomon," 123
Psalmody, 118
Psalter, 113, 124, 131; manual of private devotion, 126
Purim, feast of, 116

Qumran, community at, 149

Rachel, 16
Rankin, O. S., 164
Reconstruction, post-exilic, 101-104
Rehoboam, 49, 50, 55, 119
Religion of a closed book, 114
Revelation of God, 139, 151
Revelation of St. John Devine, 132
Robinson, T. H., 162
Rome, 154
Rowley, H. H., 157, 162, 164
Ruth, book of, 113, 116, 117, 118, 131
Rylaardson, J. C., 164

Sabbath, 99, 106
Sadducees, 149
Sagas, early Hebraic, 19
Samaria, 52, 54. See Schism, Samaritan.
Samaritans, 111
Samuel, 63
Samuel, books of, 28, 94, 112
Sarah, 60
Saul, 15, 21, 22, 23-25, 48, 53, 62, 63, 68, 69, 75, 94, 116; kingdom of, 93
Schism, the Samaritan, 112, 114
Scott, R. B. Y., 162
Sheba, 48, 53; uprising of, 50
Shechem, 16, 18, 19, 20, 34, 44, 45, 49, 109, 119; covenant at, 62; Joshua at, 43; sanctuary at, 45; site of ancient, 111; traditions of, 35, 45
Sheshbazzar, 102

Shiloh, 16, 18, 19, 20, 44, 47; destruction of, 21, 24
Simpson, C. A., 157, 159, 162
Sinai, 18, 40, 44, 157; story of, 140
Smart, J. D., 164
Smith, L. P., 164
Snaith, N. H., 159, 160
Solomon, 25, 26, 29, 48, 51, 54, 55, 69, 95, 118, 123; death of, 119
Songs, Song of, 124, 131
Sons of Israel: see Israel, sons of
Synagogue, 113
Syrians, 69, 75, 76

Taylor, Jr., C. L., 163
Temple, 26, 97, 102; dedication by Solomon, 111; destroyed by Romans, 112; see also Jerusalem
Terrien, S. L., 163, 164
Theology, covenant and law, 128; kingship, 25
Thompson, J. A., 164
Tiglath Pileser III, 160
Tigris River, 75
Torah, 126, 127; meaning of, 54
Toynbee, 30
Tribal confederacy: transition to monarchy, 21
Tyre, 52

Uriah, 25

Voegelin, Eric, 160
Von Rad, Gerhard, 159, 160, 161

Welch, A. C., 161
Wisdom ethic, 128
Wisdom Literature, 117-137, 140, 146, 147; open-mindedness of, 121; see also Wisdom ethic
Wisdom movement, 137; emphasis, 122; humanistic heritage of, 120, 122; on creation, 124; origin

of, 118; theology of, 124; theological role, 120; *see also* Job, book of

Wise men, 118, 146

Witness, biblical, 138-156; later attempts to, 115-137

Wright, G. Ernest, 157, 160, 162, 164

Yahweh: and covenant, 42, 48; and Torah, 56; prophets of, 68; purpose of, 34; religion of, 53; religion of, and Israel, 53; religion of, and Judah, 53; sovereignty of, 79; spirit of, 47

Yahwist Epic, 30; *see also* J Document

Zealots, 149

Zebulun, 157

Zechariah, 102

Zephaniah, 76

Zilpah, 157

Zimmerli, W., 165

Zophar, 128